Works for Windows

David Weale

David Weale is a lecturer in business computing at Yeovil
College in Somerset. He is the author of several books on
business computing and application programs.

DP Publications Ltd
Aldine Place
London W12 8AW

1994

Acknowledgements

This book is for my children, Becky, Sam and Chris, who all assisted with various parts of the book, and for Annette, my wife, who provided tea and sympathy. I would also like to thank my colleague Laurie Clifford, who helped with the validation of the material.

A CIP catalogue reference for this book is available from the British Library.

ISBN 185805 073 1

© David Weale 1994

Printed by The Guernsey Press Co Ltd, Vale, Guernsey CI

Preface

Who should use this book

This is a self-teaching manual that can be used by students on their own (for example within a workshop or information technology unit) or as a class text with a teacher or trainer present. It can be used for Elements 1, 2 and 3 of all five levels of the GNVQ core skill in Information Technology.

The text is easy to follow and self-explanatory and there are exercises throughout to check understanding.

The book is aimed at anyone who wants to learn to use Works for Windows quickly and effectively. It covers versions 1, 2 and 3 of the program – any substantial differences between versions are detailed in the text.

The nature of the book

The material does not assume any prior knowledge on the part of the student beyond the ability to turn the computer on and to load Windows.

This is not a program manual but a structured learning text that will help beginners learn how to use the program and how to produce effective and professional results in the minimum time.

You start learning immediately. As you do the exercises and examples using the computer, there is no lengthy material to work through before actually using the program.

You learn the commands and techniques by actually practising them step by step. It is far easier to assimilate material if it is presented in easily digestible stages.

The scope of the book

You will move from the simple to the more sophisticated levels that the program is capable of and, although there is no attempt to cover every aspect of the program, the most important and most used and useful commands and techniques are covered.

The layout and organisation of the book

The book is structured as a series of sessions building up a base of knowledge and skills. Each session is self-contained and can be completed within 40 minutes, so the book lends itself to the classroom situation and is ideal for people learning on their own.

As each activity is introduced you create your own files and documents. The files are developed through sessions and so is your use of the program. You begin with simple tasks and build up slowly and carefully to more complex tasks combining text with charts and pictures.

At the end of the book you will be able to make sensible and effective use of the features available within the program and to produce very professional-looking work.

The book is divided into five main parts:

❏ Word processing

❏ Spreadsheets

❏ Databases

❏ Microsoft Draw (and clipart library)

❏ Integration (integrating the various elements of the program).

Each part finishes with a consolidation exercise which ensures understanding and enables you to revise the preceding section before going on to the next, and at the end of the book is a final section containing seven revision exercises.

The book is organised in a logical and progressive way and you produce your own work as you advance. This will give you confidence and familiarity with the commands and techniques making up the program.

Making effective use of the book

If you follow the suggestions below you will learn more quickly and effectively.

❏ Read the instructions carefully and follow them exactly (otherwise you may achieve some rather unusual results).

❏ Practise each session until you have grasped the concepts in it and are confident before proceeding.

Unless you do this you will end up with a less than total understanding of, or skill in using, the program.

I suggest strongly that some time after you have worked through the book you return to it and go through it again.

Please remember that there is no rush to finish the book, so take it at your own speed.

Contents

An Introduction to Works

The different versions of Works for Windows

This book covers versions 1, 2 and 3 of the program. Versions 1 and 2 are very similar, version 3 has some changes. Where these are material they are described within the text.

Loading Works (versions 1 and 2)

To start Works for Windows you need to click the left-hand mouse button twice very quickly on the Works for Windows icon which looks like this:

Normally the icon will be in the WINDOWS APPLICATIONS group window, but it may be in a different group (depending upon how your system has been set up).

After loading Works for Windows you will be presented with the following dialog box. To select one of the items simply click the left hand mouse button on your choice.

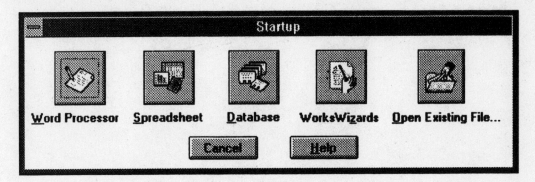

Loading Works (version 3)

To start Works for Windows you need to click the left-hand mouse button twice very quickly on the Works for Windows icon which looks like this:

The start up screen differs from the other versions and is shown below.

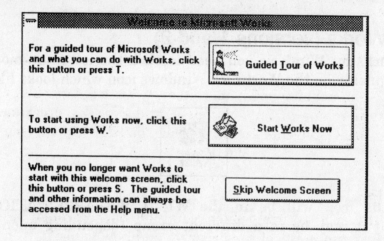

Assuming you click on the START WORKS NOW button, you will see the main Works screen which you will return to periodically while you use the program.

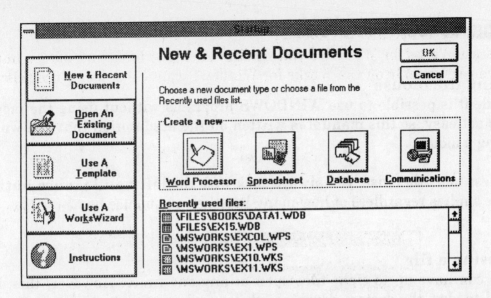

As you can see this dialog box is merely an extended version of the start-up dialog box that is shown for versions 1 and 2 of the program. You can access the tutorial from this screen or from the HELP menu (see below).

The tutorial

WORKS contains a tutorial which you can work through to familiarise yourself with the contents of the program and how to use it.

The tutorial explains the program and allows a limited practice in using the commands. It is an overview and should be treated as such. You can usefully spend anything from half an hour to several hours familiarising yourself with the program features, depending upon your previous experience and aptitude.

Everyone will benefit from working through the tutorial, especially if this is the first integrated program you have used or you are unfamiliar with any of the parts of it.

Initial concepts in Works

Using the mouse

While it is possible to use WINDOWS programs without using the mouse, it is not easy, so this manual is written on the assumption that you will be using a mouse.

Unless told otherwise, you always click with the **left-hand mouse button**. This applies regardless of how many buttons your mouse has.

Closing a file

You can have up to eight files open at any one time. However, this does tend to slow the system down, so when you have finished with a file pull down the FILE menu by clicking on the word FILE along the top of the screen and then select CLOSE by clicking on it.

Closing down completely

When you have finished with WORKS click the mouse in the top left-hand corner of the screen (on the symbol shown below) and you will be able to choose CLOSE from the menu that appears (by clicking the mouse on the word CLOSE).

Help

As with most WINDOWS programs help is easily available (the help is context-sensitive; this means that the help given will be relevant to the problem). To activate the help screens simply press the **F1** key.

For example, if you have selected the EDIT menu and want help on PASTE SPECIAL, then move the cursor (using the cursor keys) to the topic and press **F1**. The HELP screen on this topic will appear.

You can also search through the Help screens. Start by pressing the function key **F1** and, as you can see from the screen below, there is a button called **Search**.

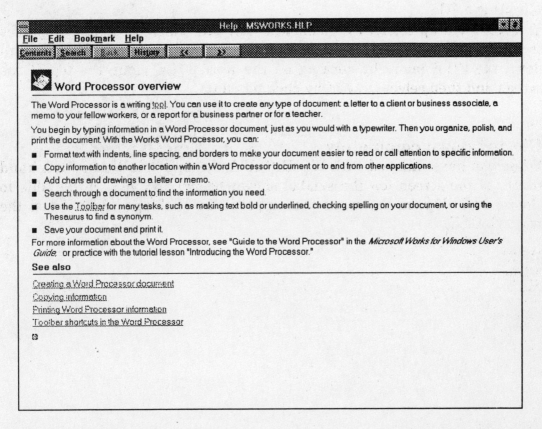

Click the mouse on this and then enter the word or phrase you want help on. Then, from the range of possible topics, choose one by selecting it with the mouse (or cursor keys).

Click on the button SHOW TOPICS and again select the topic you want and click on the GO TO button.

Having this kind of help available is enormously useful as it avoids the need to use the program manual too often and it is fast and effective.

To close down the HELP screen click on the

symbol and choose CLOSE.

Using the keyboard

Most of the keys are self-explanatory, but below is a summary of the less obvious ones.

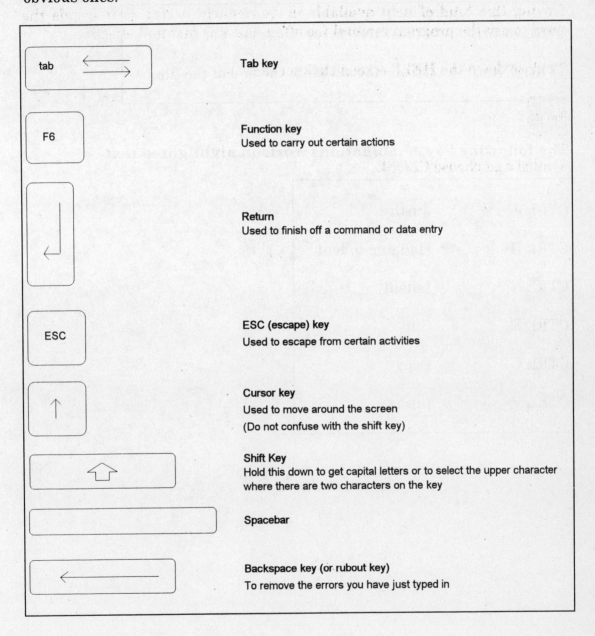

Tab key

Function key
Used to carry out certain actions

Return
Used to finish off a command or data entry

ESC (escape) key
Used to escape from certain activities

Cursor key
Used to move around the screen
(Do not confuse with the shift key)

Shift Key
Hold this down to get capital letters or to select the upper character where there are two characters on the key

Spacebar

Backspace key (or rubout key)
To remove the errors you have just typed in

Key combinations
The key combinations that you will find useful for speed of working are:

CTRL HOME	Moves the cursor to the start of the file
CTRL END	Moves the cursor to the end of the file

The following key combinations work on highlighted text

CTRL J	Justify
CTRL H	Hanging indent
CTRL N	Indent
CTRL X	Cut
CTRL C	Copy
CTRL V	Insert

Word Processing

Starting off

Word processing is the most popular application of computers and the one which most people are familiar with. It is the entering, manipulation and presentation of text and using a computer allows a far more sophisticated approach to this.

Text can be moved around and errors corrected easily, different styles and sizes of text can be used, and layout can be altered without difficulty. Spelling can be checked, and the built-in thesaurus can be used to find alternative words.

Most word processing programs also allow you to incorporate charts and pictures into your work.

As a result of the facilities offered by word processors, and the ability to save documents on disk to be recalled at any time, word processors have more-or-less replaced typewriters in the business world.

The word processing section of the manual contains the following sessions:

First things

To begin you are going to create a new Word Processing file, so click on the Word Processing icon with the left hand mouse button and you will have opened up a word processing file.

The word processing screen looks like this:

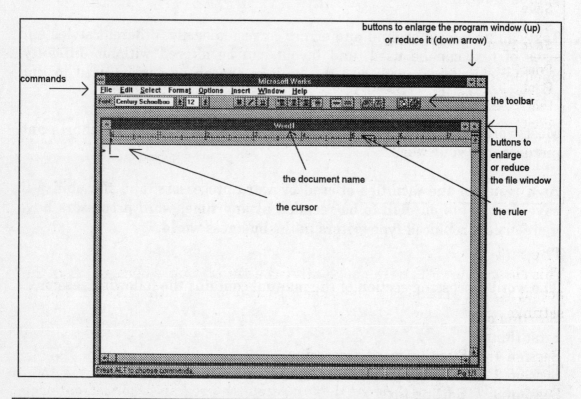

The toolbar and menus for version 3 of the program are slightly different, the menus are arranged in a different sequence and there are changes to the buttons on the toolbar. Significant changes are identified in the text.

One of the new features of version 3 is that when you position the mouse pointer over any button on the toolbar, after a few moments the name or function of the button is displayed. You need never worry about forgetting the name of any button with version 3.

Commands

These are PULL DOWN MENUS from which you can select various commands by clicking the mouse on the chosen command; an example is shown below (the FILE menu).

Create New File...
Open Existing File...
Close
Save   Ctrl+S
Save As...
Save Workspace
Print Preview
Print...   Ctrl+P
Print Form Letters...
Print Labels...
Page Setup & Margins...
Printer Setup...
Exit Works

The ruler

This shows the width of the page **after** the margins have been set, thus the actual typing area across the page. It also displays the tab and indent settings (of which more later).

The document name

This will show WORD1 as the default when the program is loaded but once you open a file or save a file then the name will alter to the actual name of the file.

The toolbar (versions 1 and 2)

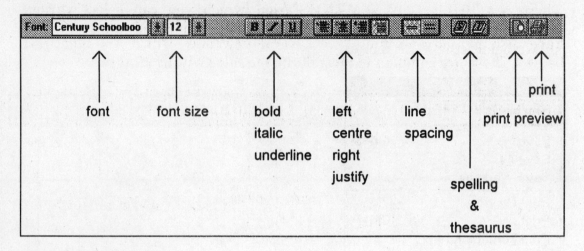

Fonts and Font Size
There are different designs of type, known as fonts, and fonts are available in different sizes. The number and variety available will depend upon your system.

Bold, Italic, Underline
Any or all of these can be used.

Left, Centre, Right, Justify
The way the text is aligned on the page.

Line Spacing
This can be either single or double.

Spelling and Thesaurus
You will want to spell check your work and to use the thesaurus to find alternative words.

Print Preview
You can see how your work will look before printing it out (and thereby saving effort and paper).

Print
When you are sure about the layout etc. you can print out the material.

The toolbar (versions 3)

As you can see there are differences between the toolbars, some buttons have disappeared and there are several new ones which are identified below. These are common to most of the modules within Works.

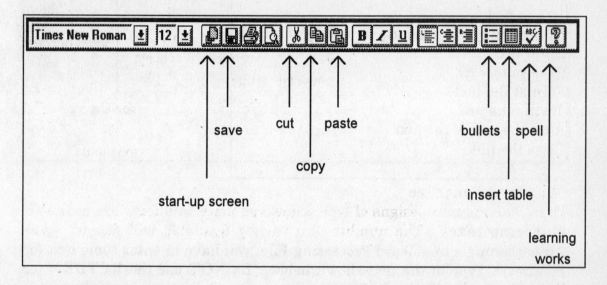

Session 1: Starting word processing

Objectives

By the end of this session you will be able to :
Enter text
Save your work
Format the text
Justify the text
Alter the size of the text
Close the file

Entering text

After opening a new Word Processing File, you have to enter some text (or pictures). Type in the text shown below. Do **NOT** use the **RETURN** (or Enter) key **until the end of the paragraph** and do not worry if the text is not displayed exactly as shown below (for example you may be using a different font).

Word Processing lets you enter, edit and format your text so that it has a professional look to it. Word Processing has several major advantages over typewriters as it lets you alter the text, add to it, delete words or lines. You can put key words or phrases in bold, italic or underline them. You can justify the text. Also you can check your spelling (very useful).

Now you want to add a title, so move the cursor to the top left of the screen and press the **RETURN** key, which will leave a gap at the top of the document. Move the cursor into that gap and type the following.

What is Word Processing ?

Now press the **RETURN** key to leave a gap between the title and the text.

Saving your work

One of the most important aspects of computing is to save your work **often** as computer systems can go wrong and if you have not saved your work you may lose it if something does go wrong.

To save documents within WORKS simply click the cursor on the FILE command (along the top of the screen) and then click on the command SAVE AS.

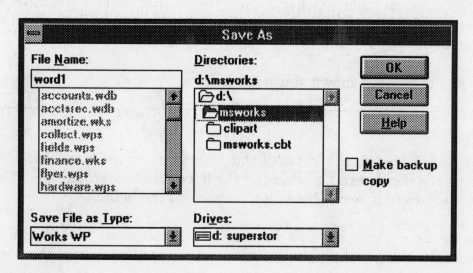

> **Notes :**
> The files etc. shown above may differ from those on your system so do not worry about this.
>
> Version 3 of the program has a slightly different dialog box.

Click the mouse within the **File Name** box and while holding the mouse button down, drag the mouse across the existing file name (WORD1) so that it is highlighted. You can then type the name you wish to give to the file up to eight characters are allowed but these should not include any spaces or full stops.

Call this file **EX1**

Then click on the **OK** button in the dialog box.

You may notice that the program automatically adds **.WPS** after the name. This is called the file extension and shows that it is a WORKS word processing file (most programs automatically add their particular extensions).

The new file name is shown above the text.

> **Notes :**
> In the dialog box, to the right of the File name is the word Directories. This lets you decide exactly where on the hard disc to store the file. Unless you want to store it somewhere else, just accept the default.
>
> Below the Directories box is a Drives box. If you want to alter the drive you are saving on then simply click on the arrow to the right of the box and then click on the drive you want to save the file on, e.g. **a:** if you want to save to a floppy disc in drive A:

Formatting your work

To make the heading stand out, you are going to format it to bold. To do this click the mouse button at the start or end of the heading and (still holding the mouse button down) drag the mouse so that all the heading is highlighted.

Now simply click the mouse on the bold symbol in the toolbar (shown below).

The text will now be in bold.

To remove highlighting click the mouse outside of the highlighted area.

Justifying the text

Personally I like text to be justified as I think it makes the layout much cleaner and the text easier to read.

To justify your text highlight it (click and drag the mouse) and then click on the justify symbol in the toolbar (shown below) or use the quick keys by holding down the CTRL key while pressing the J key.

In version 3 the justification button has disappeared from the toolbar and you will need to use the CTRL and J keys to justify the text.

You will see that the text now has a straight right hand margin - this is justified.

Increasing the size of the text

You can alter the size of the text by clicking on the arrow to the right of the Size Box in the toolbar and selecting a different size. A selection of sizes should appear and you can use the arrows that appear to scroll up and down the range of sizes (sizes of characters are in points; each point represents roughly 1/72 inch).

In this case, after highlighting the title, select a number four sizes larger (i.e. if the original is 12 point then choose 16 point).

Finishing Off

The screen should look similar to the one shown below.

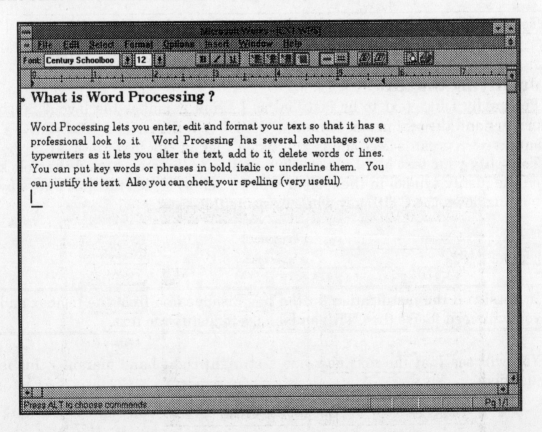

Save your file as EX1 again. If you are asked whether to replace the existing file answer OK. Then close the file (FILE CLOSE).

Session 2: Adding text and formatting

Objectives

By the end of this session you will be able to :
Open a file
Add text to a file
Format both text and paragraphs

Opening a file

Opening a file is very similar to saving it. You click on the FILE command and then OPEN EXISTING FILE. A dialog box will appear which looks similar to that shown below.

In version 3, you can click on the OPEN AN EXISTING DOCUMENT button or you can select one of the listed files in the lower section of the dialog box.

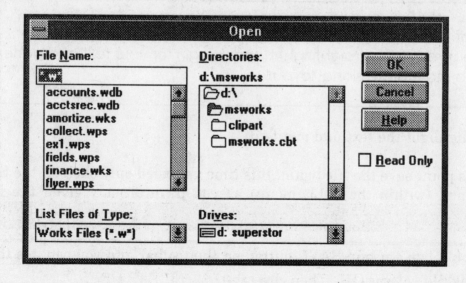

You can either type in the File Name, in this case (**EX1**), or click on it within the box showing the file names (remember that you can scroll through this list by using the arrows to the right of the box).

Then click on the **OK** symbol within the dialog box.

Note:
Again you have a choice of Directories and Drives and you may need to select different ones to those shown.

Adding Text

Once you have opened up the file you can change the contents of it.

You are going to add a new paragraph to the original. Position the cursor at the end of the text by clicking the mouse or using the cursor keys (you may need to press the RETURN key once or twice to create space).

Now enter the following text.

One of the most useful formatting commands is that of justification, which gives you a straight right hand margin for your text and generally gives a more professional layout.

Now highlight the text and justify it.

At this point save the file again; this time you need only click on the SAVE command (within the FILE menu) as you have already given the file a name.

Version 3 has a useful SAVE button on the toolbar and you can use this to save the file.

Note:
The difference between SAVE AS and SAVE is that SAVE AS always prompts you for a file name so that you can change it if you wish, SAVE saves the file under the original name.

Now add a further paragraph below the one you have just typed in (remember that the RETURN key can be used to create spaces).

Other useful facilities are being able to preview your work before printing it and being able to spell check your work so that the reader is not presented with poor spelling.

Justify the paragraph and save the file (without changing its name).

The final result should look like this.

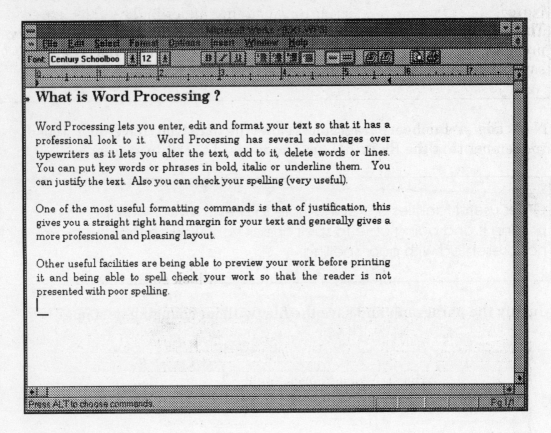

More on character formatting

So far you have learnt how to put words into bold type.

Now put the words *Word Processing* into italic (but only the two instances within the text, not the title.).

Also put the words **justification** and **preview** into bold.

Paragraph formatting

As well as character formatting (bold, italic, underlining, fonts) you can alter the look of the text by changing the layout (as you did when you justified the text).

You are going to centre the heading.

To do this position the cursor somewhere on that line and then click the centre symbol in the toolbar (shown below).

The title should now be centred.

Save the file as EX1 and close it. It should now look similar to this.

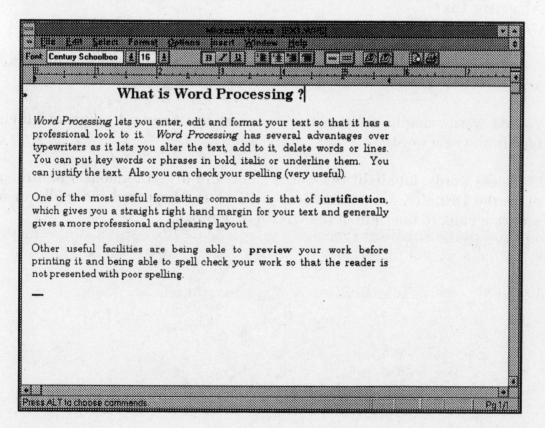

Session 3: Editing text

Objectives

By the end of this session you will be able to :
Alter text
Move text
Copy text
Add headers and footers
Preview your work

Altering text
Open the file EX1.

After having entered your text you may wish to change, add or to delete words.

To add words simply position the cursor at the required point and then type in the new words.

To delete words, highlight the words (click and drag the mouse) and then press the DELETE key (marked as such on the keyboard, normally in a separate bank to the right of the QWERTY keys).

Delete the word

> major

in the second line of the first paragraph.

Add the words

> and pleasing

between the last two words of the second paragraph (so that it reads as shown below).

> professional and pleasing layout

Moving text around a document

This is easy and very useful. You are going to move the second and third paragraphs around.

To do this, highlight the second paragraph and then pull down the EDIT menu and select CUT.

Now position the cursor below the third paragraph (you may need to press the RETURN key to create space), pull down the EDIT menu again and select PASTE.

> If there is too much space between paragraphs, move the cursor into the space and press the DELETE key to remove unwanted spaces.

The paragraphs will now have been switched around as can be seen below.

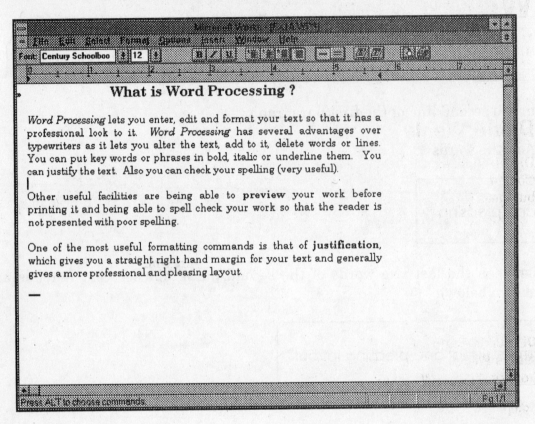

Copying text

If you want to copy material rather than move it around, then highlight the text, choose EDIT and COPY, then position the cursor and choose EDIT and PASTE.

Copy the second paragraph (as shown in the screen above) below the third paragraph (so that there are four paragraphs in total).

Delete the second paragraph.

Adding Headers and Footers

It is very useful, and indeed professional, to add headers and/or footers to your document. These are text that repeats itself at the top or bottom of every page.

An example of a footer could be page numbers, and an example of a header might be the chapter name, your name or the name of the report.

To add headers and/or footers, pull down the EDIT menu and select HEADERS & FOOTERS.

In version 3 you use the VIEW menu which contains the HEADERS & FOOTERS command.

Click on USE HEADER & FOOTER PARAGRAPHS so that the little box has an X in it. Then click on OK and you will see two lines appear at the top of your document.

The footer is already set up as the page number, the header is blank so that you can add your own text (you can delete the page numbering if you wish and add anything you want as a footer).

This time add your name as the header, format it to italic and use a font two points smaller than the remainder of the text; leave the footer as it is.

Note:
You will only be able to see the headers and footers properly when previewing the text (see below).

Previewing

When you want to print your work it is always best to preview it first so that you can see precisely how it will look.

To do this you click on the preview symbol in the toolbar (as shown below).

You should see a screen which looks like this.

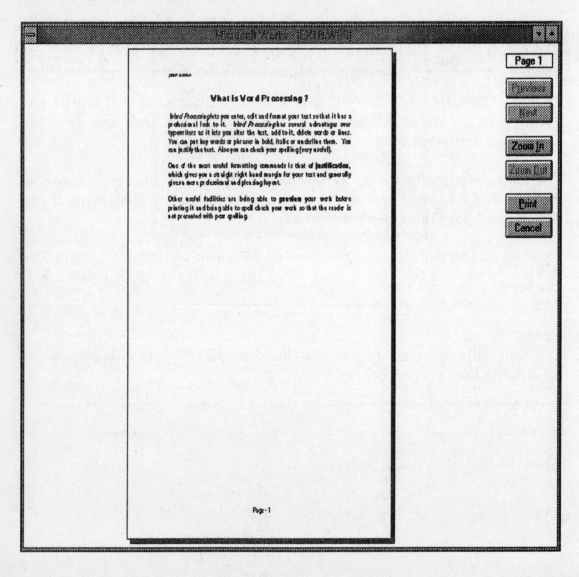

Note :
You can click on the symbols shown on the right of the screen to move to the next page, zoom in or out, print the document or cancel when you want to return to the original.

When you are happy with the preview click on the FILE menu and select PRINT.

A dialog box will appear (version 3 is slightly different).

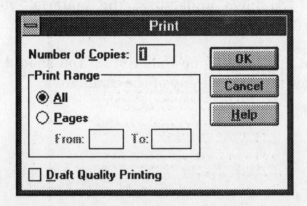

This lets you select the number of copies and print only those pages from the whole document that you want to. Click on OK.

Note:
To select only certain pages, click on Pages and a large dot will appear to the left of the word, then click within the **From** box and enter the page you want to start from. Do the same for the **To** box and then click on **OK**.

Save the file as EX1 and then close it.

Session 4: Exercise

```
┌─────────────────────────────────────────────────────────┐
│                                                         │
│  Objectives                                             │
│                                                         │
│  To revise the work that has been done so far.          │
│                                                         │
└─────────────────────────────────────────────────────────┘
```

This is the first of many exercises throughout the book. Its purpose is to make sure that you have understood the material you have worked through so far and that you can apply it to your own work.

This is **not** a test and there is no time limit. You should look back if you have forgotten how to carry out any of the commands.

Tasks

1. Create a new word processing file.

2. Enter the following text. Do not worry if it does not look exactly the same yet.

So far you have learnt the basic elements of word processing. You have created a new file, entered text into it, saved the file and printed it.

You have also learnt about both character and paragraph formatting, remember that character formatting means putting characters into bold, italic, underlining or changing the font size or type. Paragraph formatting can be used to justify the text. Later on you will learn how to align the text and how to double line space.

Other commands you have covered are headers and footers and moving text around a document. Also you have dealt with adding and deleting text.

3. Justify the text.

4. Add a title and leave a blank line between the title and the text.

Exercise One

5. Format the title to bold, put it in a font size four points larger than the rest of the text and centre it.

6. Swap the second and third paragraphs around.

7.   Add a header with your name (format it to italic and size it two points smaller than the rest of the text) and a footer for the page number (again size it two points smaller than the rest of the text).

8.   Preview it and if it is satisfactory print it out.

The end result in preview should look like this.

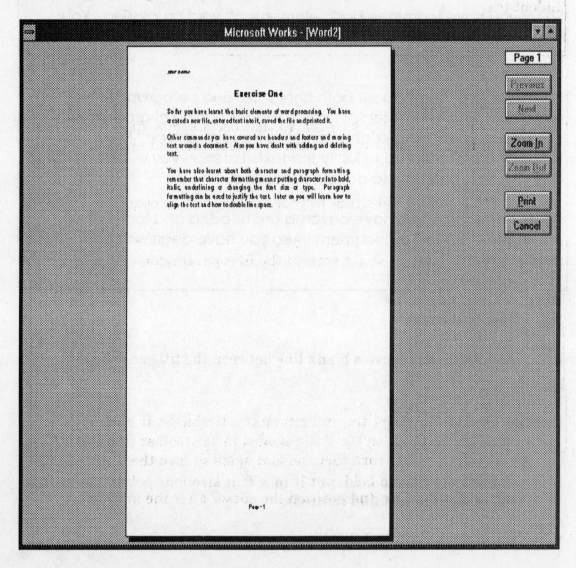

9.   Save the file as **EX2** and then close it.

Session 5: Indenting and aligning

Objectives

By the end of this session you will be able to :
Indent text
Align text

Indenting

You may want to indent your work so that certain text stands out within the page or if you want to use numbered paragraphs (for example within a report).

You are going to add indenting to your original file so open the file called **EX1**.

Now position the cursor at the start of the first paragraph.

Type in the figure

1.

Note how it has retained the italic format. Highlight it and remove the italic format by clicking on the italic symbol in the toolbar (the symbols act as toggles - click once to turn them on and again to turn them off).

Remove the highlighting and position the cursor after the number.

Press the **TAB** key and the rest of the first line will have moved across by half an inch.

To create a hanging indent simply hold down the **CTRL** key and, while doing so, press the **H** key (H for hanging indent).

You have now created an indented paragraph.

Note :

You **must** use this technique otherwise you will not be able to justify the text. Please do **not** tab each line - only the very first line of each paragraph needs to be tabbed, the other lines of each paragraph are indented automatically when you use **CTRL** and **H**.

Now number and indent the remaining paragraphs.

The end result should look similar to this when previewed.

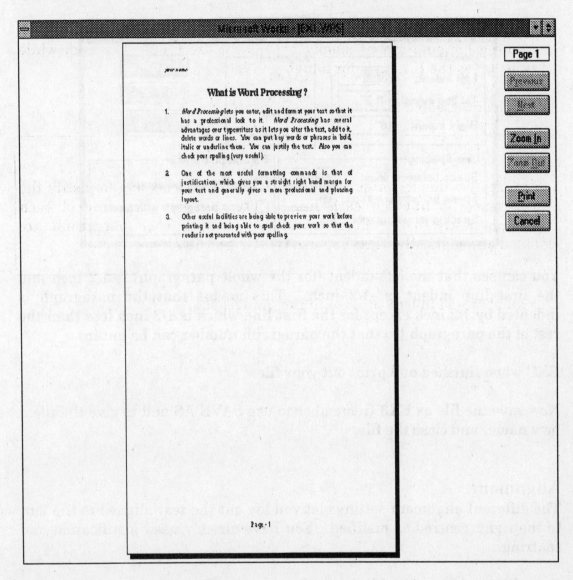

Now, so you can see precisely what you have done, position the cursor within any of the paragraphs. Then click on the command FORMAT and then INDENTS & SPACING.

In version 3 the sequence is FORMAT, PARAGRAPH and then INDENTS and ALIGNMENT.

You should see the following dialog box appear.

You can see that the left indent (for the whole paragraph) is 1/2 inch and the first line indent is -1/2 inch. This means that the paragraph is indented by 1/2 inch except for the first line which is 1/2 inch less than the rest of the paragraph (so that the paragraph number can be put in).

ESC when finished and print out your file.

Now save the file as **EX3** (remember to use SAVE AS and to give the file a new name) and close the file.

Alignment
The different alignment settings let you lay out the text aligned to the left, to the right, centred or justified. You have already used justification and centring.

Open **EX1** again and highlight the first paragraph.

Select the right alignment symbol in the toolbar and the whole paragraph will be right aligned.

Highlight the second paragraph and then select the left alignment symbol in the toolbar and the whole paragraph will be left aligned.

Highlight the third paragraph and then select the centre alignment symbol in the toolbar and the whole paragraph will be centred.

The final result when previewed should look like this.

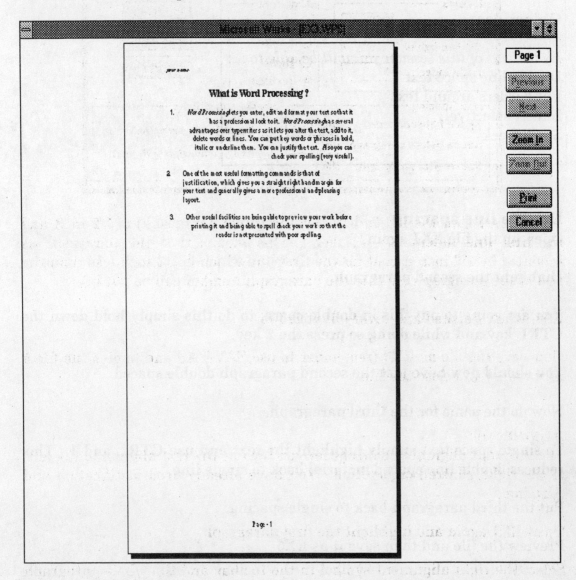

After previewing your work, print it out and save the file as **EX4** and close the file.

Session 6: Layout and spell checking

Objectives

By the end of this session you will be able to :
Double line space text
Put borders around text
Indent selectively
Spell check

Double line spacing
Open up the file **EX1** again.

Highlight the second paragraph.

You are going to put this in double space; to do this simply hold down the **CTRL** key and while doing so press the **2** key.

You should now have just the second paragraph double spaced.

Now do the same for the third paragraph.

To single space text simply highlight the text and use **CTRL** and **1**. This reduces double line spaced material back to single line.

Put the third paragraph back to single spacing.

Preview the file and then save it as **EX5**.

Borders

It is often useful to put borders around part(s) of your document; this can make material stand out and tends to draw the reader's attention to it.

You are going to put a border around the third paragraph.

Note :
Make sure that there is at least one blank line below the highlighted material you are creating a border around.

Highlight the paragraph and then select FORMAT and then BORDER from the command menu. You will see the following dialog box appear.

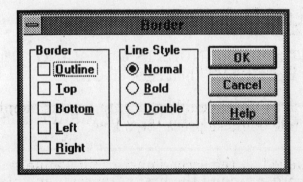

Ensure that you have clicked on OUTLINE (so that there is a cross in the box to the left of the word) and then click on BOLD.

Finally click on OK and you should have a bold border around the third paragraph.

Now put a double line border around the first paragraph.

To remove a border, highlight the material within the border and then select from the commands FORMAT and BORDER.

Click on the item under border which has a cross in the box next to it; the cross will disappear. Make sure that there is **nothing** shown in any of the boxes in the border column of the dialog box, then click on OK and the border should have disappeared.

Remove the border around the third paragraph.

Preview the file and then save it (as **EX5** again).

More on indents

So far you have indented by using a hanging indent, now you are going to look at normal paragraph indenting to see the other effects you can produce.

Using the current file (**EX5**), highlight the second paragraph.

Click on FORMAT and then INDENTS & SPACING. This time enter 1" left indent and 1" right indent, then click on OK.

In version 3 the sequence is FORMAT, PARAGRAPH and then INDENTS and ALIGNMENT.

Now remove the border around the first paragraph and place a bold border round paragraph two.

The end result when previewed will look like this.

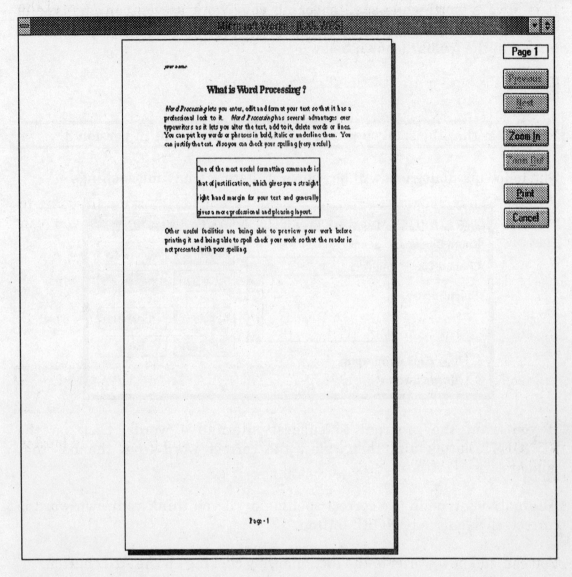

As you can see the second paragraph has been double spaced, indented and has a border around it. It certainly attracts the reader's attention (be careful not to overdo the special effects though).

Now save the file (again as **EX5**) and print the file.

Spell checking

It is always worthwhile spell checking your work as you can mis-type or misspell words. To check your spelling and typing accuracy click on the **S** button in the toolbar (shown below).

Remember that the spell checking button looks different in version 3.

The following dialog box will be shown if there are any misspellings.

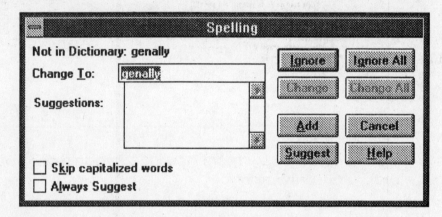

If you want the program to suggest alternative words, click on the SUGGEST button and then select the correct word from the list that appears.

Alternatively type in the correct spelling or, if you think your own word is correct, click on the IGNORE button.

You can add new words to the dictionary by clicking on the ADD button.

Now close the file after saving the corrections (as EX5).

Session 7: Page breaks and revision

Objectives

By the end of this session you will be able to :
Do a revision exercise
Put page breaks in your work

Exercise
Create a new word processing file.

Enter the following text.

As you have seen, the use of alignment and indents can make your work more effective and interesting.

Always remember though that you are trying to communicate and that the computer and the programs you use are merely a method of doing this.

Another useful tool is being able to place a border around material and being able to double space any or all of your work.

It is best to keep the layout as simple as possible as trying to be too clever can destroy the effect you want to create.

If you justify your work, make sure you justify it all, and not to leave part of it justified and part unjustified.

Justify all the text.

Enter the heading 'Layout' and RETURN twice (so that there is a gap between the heading and the remainder of the text).

Format the title to bold, centre it and alter the size to two points larger than the rest of the text.

Use the hanging indent technique to add paragraph numbers to each of the paragraphs.

Right align the second paragraph.

Indent the third paragraph 1" left and 1" right (leave the first line indent as -0.5").

Double space the fifth paragraph.

Place a double line border around the fourth paragraph.

Add a header to your work with your name in it, format the header to bold and size it two points smaller than the rest of the text. Right align the header.

Have the page number as the footer, format it to italic and size it two points smaller than the rest of the text.

Spell check your work.

Preview the file which should look like this.

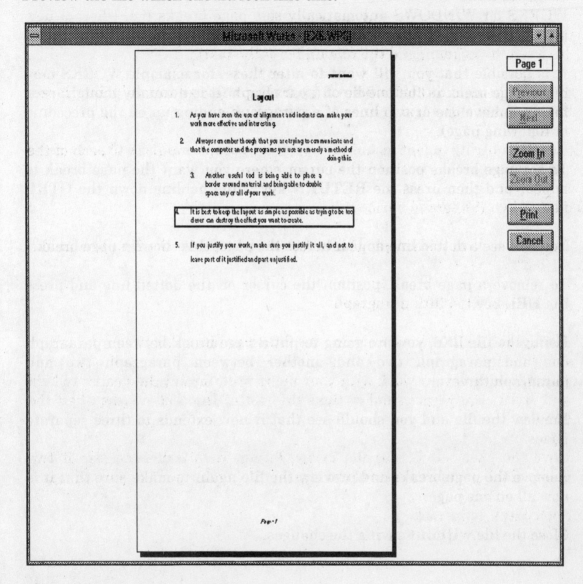

Print it out and save it as **EX6**.

Page Breaks

WORKS for WINDOWS automatically sets page breaks (i.e. where a new page starts when you print out).

It is possible that you will want to alter these, for example WORKS may put a page break in the middle of a paragraph (it is normally thought poor layout to have one or two lines of a paragraph ending up on the preceding or following page).

To set page breaks position the cursor where you want the page break to appear and then press the **RETURN** key while holding down the **CTRL** key.

You will see a dotted line appear across the page, this shows a page break.

To remove a page break, position the cursor on the dotted line and press the **DEL** key.

Using the file EX6, you are going to put a page break between paragraph one and paragraph two and another between paragraph two and paragraph three.

Preview the file and you should see that it now extends to three separate pages.

Remove the page breaks and preview the file again to make sure that it is now all on one page.

Close the file **without** saving the changes.

Session 8: Graphics

Objectives

By the end of this session you will be able to :
Add pictures to your text

Adding graphics to your work
There is a saying that

'A picture adds a thousand words'.

The primary reason for any form of business computing is to communicate something from one person to another. If this communication can be assisted by the use of pictures, graphs, charts or any other form of graphics then they should be used where possible.

Note :
Be careful though, as it is easy to include pictures for the sake of it, which may not be relevant or sensible within the context and can actually detract from the end result.

Now you are going to produce something very different, a publicity sheet for a forthcoming auction.

Create a new word processing file and enter the following heading.

FOR SALE

Format the text to ARIAL size 30 point and centre it.

RETURN three times and then add the text

Desirable Town Residence

RETURN four times after typing this.

Format the text to ARIAL size 24 point, centre it and put a border around it.

You will see that the border stretches across the page, it is possible to indent this.

Highlight the title and pull down the FORMAT menu and then select INDENTS & SPACING.

In version 3 the sequence is FORMAT, PARAGRAPH and then INDENTS and ALIGNMENT.

Enter indents of 0.8 inches left and right (if this doesn't look quite right then alter the figures as necessary).

Move the cursor to the bottom line and pull down the INSERT menu. Then select DRAWING and the MICROSOFT DRAW screen will appear (as shown below).

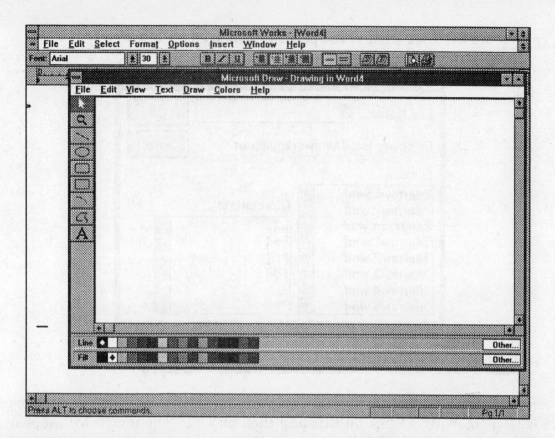

MICROSOFT DRAW lets you create your own artwork or import predrawn art (clipart). You are going to use a predrawn image that comes with the program.

To do so click on the command FILE (within the MICROSOFT DRAW window) and select IMPORT PICTURE).

You will be presented with a dialog box and you should double click quickly on the word CLIPART that will appear within the Directories box.

You should then see a list of the predrawn images (as below).

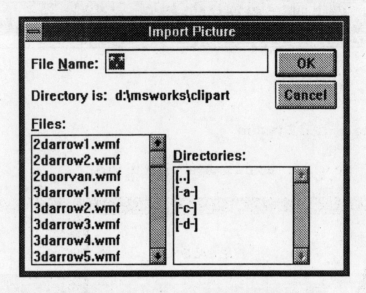

Version 3 has a totally different set of clipart images.

Scroll down the list (using the arrows) until you see the one called VICHOUSE.WMF. Click on this and then on OK. The image will appear within MICROSOFT DRAW.

If you are using version 3 of the program I suggest you choose PHONE.WMF.

To place this within your document click on FILE (within the MICROSOFT DRAW window) and then on EXIT AND RETURN TO WORD1 (or whatever the file is called) and then YES to UPDATE WORD1.

The picture should now appear in your document and should be centred.

Position the cursor to the right of the picture and RETURN six times, then type the following.

> Phone 345-987-2345

Format this to ARIAL 24 point.

Preview your file which should look similar to this.

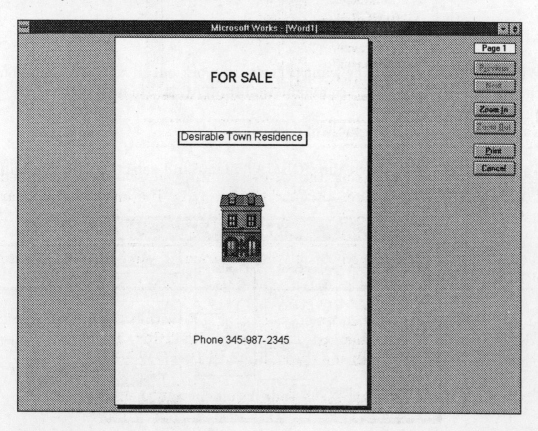

Print the file and save it as **EX7.**

Close the file.

Session 9: Tabs

Objectives

By the end of this session you will be able to :
Use tabs

Create a new word processing file.

When you create a table or want to lay your work out in columns then you can use the FORMAT TAB command and the TAB key to help you.

You are going to create a table of data.

To set the tabs, pull down the FORMAT menu and select TABS; you will see the following dialog box appear.

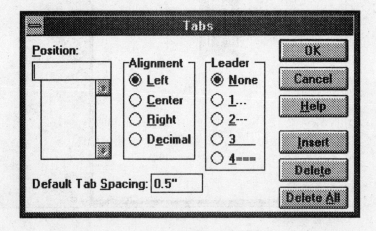

Click within the Position box and enter the figure **1.5**, then click on the INSERT button. This inserts a tab stop 1.5" from the left.

Set another tab for 4", only this time click on DECIMAL first as this is to be a decimal tab (so that numbers line up underneath each other), and then click on INSERT.

When you have finished click on OK; you will see the tab stops displayed on the ruler.

Enter the following data. You **must** press the TAB key to move across the page from one column to the next and then the RETURN key to move onto the next line.

Make	Model	Cost
Kona	Fire Mountain	459
Kona	Cinder Cone	699
Trek	830	299
Trek	930	449
Trek	930sh	599
Trek	9000	1199
Specialised	Rockhopper	499
Specialised	Hard Rock	349

Format the headings to bold and underlined (you will need to highlight each word separately to underline the words but not the intervening spaces).

Add your name as a header (aligned to the centre) and include the page number as the footer.

Preview the file.

The file should look like this.

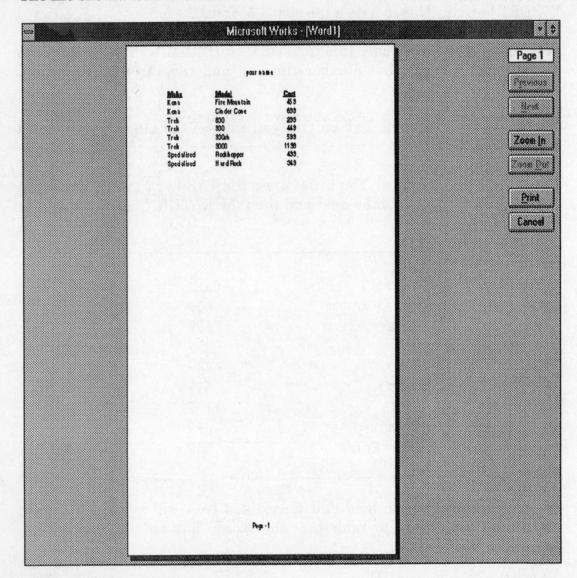

Save it as **EX8**, print it and close it.

Session 10: Revision

Objectives

To revise the material on TABS you have covered so far.

Exercise

Create a new word processing file.

Set tabs at the positions shown below.

2"	centre
3.5"	decimal
5"	decimal

Set out the following table using tabs.

Name	No. in stock	Cost	Sale price
Nike Air Max	12	34.32	59.99
Nike Skylon	6	25.21	49.95
Nike Jordans	3	45.32	79.99
Asics 101	8	32.12	49.99
Asics Saga	1	19.99	32.99

Format the headings to italic and bold.

Enter your name as a header and format this as you wish; leave the footer as it is.

Preview the file and print it out.

The final result should look like this.

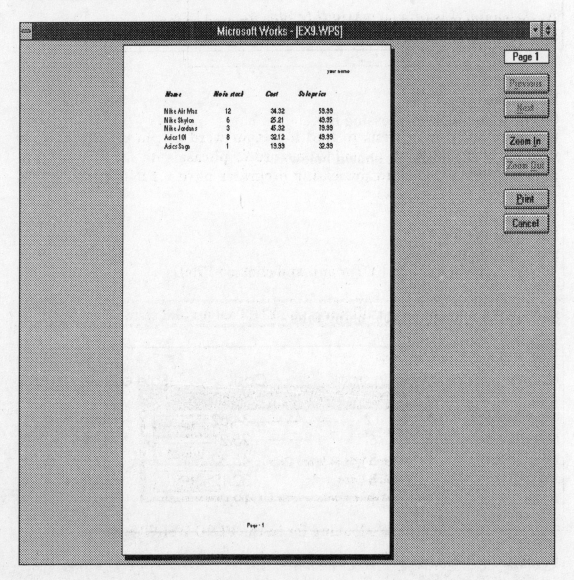

Save the file as **EX8A** and close it.

Session 11: Find and replace

Objectives

By the end of this session you will be able to :
Find and replace text

Find

Sometimes you may want to find a certain word or phrase within your work, or you may wish to replace a word or phrase with another word or phrase. To do this word processing programs have a FIND & REPLACE feature.

Open the file **EX1**.

Now pull down the SELECT menu and click on FIND.

In version 3 you need to pull down the EDIT menu and then select FIND.

You will see a dialog box.

You type the word you are looking for in the FIND WHAT box.

Notes :
You must make sure that the cursor is at the start of your document before beginning this process.

MATCH WHOLE WORD ONLY   If you select this by clicking on the box so that an **X** appears then your word or phrase will only be found if it is a whole word i.e. it is not part of a word, e.g. man in the word woman.

MATCH CASE   If you select this then only an exact match of upper and lower case letters will be found.

For this example enter the word in the FIND WHAT box.

it

then click on MATCH WHOLE WORD ONLY, and then click on OK.

The first occurrence of the word will be found (note how only whole words are found, not instances where it is part of another word).

Note :
Use the **F7** key to repeat the search as many times as you want to.

Repeat the search until you get to the end of the file. At the end of the file a dialog box will appear (shown below) which means that there are no more occurrences of that word.

Note :
To get to the top or bottom of your file quickly use **CTRL** and **HOME** or
CTRL and **END**)

Now go back to the top of the file and repeat the search for the word below
(this time selecting MATCH CASE as well).

you

Replace
This is very similar to FIND only this time you can replace the words you
find. The dialog box is shown below.

Replace	
Find What: [　　　　　]	Replace
Replace With: [　　　　　]	Replace All
☐ Match Whole Word Only	Cancel
☐ Match Case	Help

The dialog box for version 3 is slightly different but follows the same
general idea.

As you can see there are some extra buttons on the right of the dialog box.

REPLACE WITH allows you to enter the word you want to substitute, REPLACE lets you choose whether to replace each occurrence of the word, and if you select REPLACE ALL then all the occurrences of the word will be replaced without the computer prompting you.

Go to the top of the file and replace the word

you

with the word

me

Choose MATCH WHOLE WORD ONLY and MATCH CASE and then click on REPLACE. You will be asked whether you want to replace each time the word is found. You need to click on one of the boxes. In this case always choose YES.

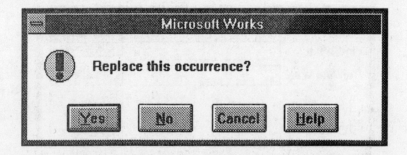

Now close the file **without** saving it.

Session 12: Word count, margins and non-printing characters

Objectives

By the end of this session you will be able to :
Count the number of words in a document
Alter the margins and page size
Display non-printing characters

Counting the number of words

Both journalists and students find it extremely useful to be able to count the number of words in a document.

To do this open **EX1** again and then click on OPTIONS and WORD COUNT. You should see the following dialog box (do not worry if the number of words is slightly different).

> In version 3 choose TOOLS and then WORD COUNT.

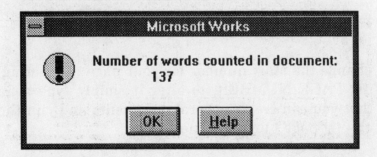

Now save the file and close it.

Page setup and margins
This time open the file EX3.

Quite often you will want to alter the page margins and sometimes the page size. To do this pull down the FILE menu and select PAGE SETUP & MARGINS.

For version choose FILE and then PAGE SETUP.

You will see the following dialog box.

```
┌─────────────────────────────────────────────────┐
│ ─            Page Setup & Margins                │
│                                                   │
│  Top margin:    [1"]    Page length: [11"]   ┌──────┐ │
│                                               │  OK  │ │
│  Bottom margin: [1"]    Page width:  [8.5"]  └──────┘ │
│                                               ┌────────┐│
│  Left margin:   [1.25"]                       │ Cancel ││
│                                               └────────┘│
│  Right margin:  [1.25"]  1st page number: [1] ┌──────┐ │
│                                               │ Help │ │
│  Header margin: [0.5"]                        └──────┘ │
│                                                   │
│  Footer margin: [0.75"]                           │
└─────────────────────────────────────────────────┘
```

It is likely that you will want to change the page length and width to A4 (11.69" x 8.27"), if it hasn't already been changed.

Version 3 choose SOURCE, SIZE and ORIENTATION.

Note :
It is easy to change the start number for your page numbering as you can see the box 1st PAGE NUMBER; to alter it simply type a new number. This means that you can create several documents and join them together by changing the 1st page number as necessary.

In version 3 this is found within OTHER OPTIONS part of PAGE SETUP.

Change the margins to those shown below.

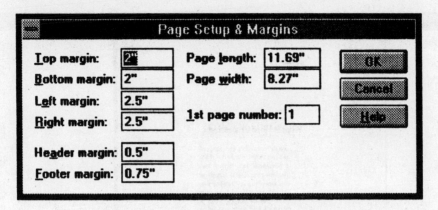

Then preview your work which should look like this.

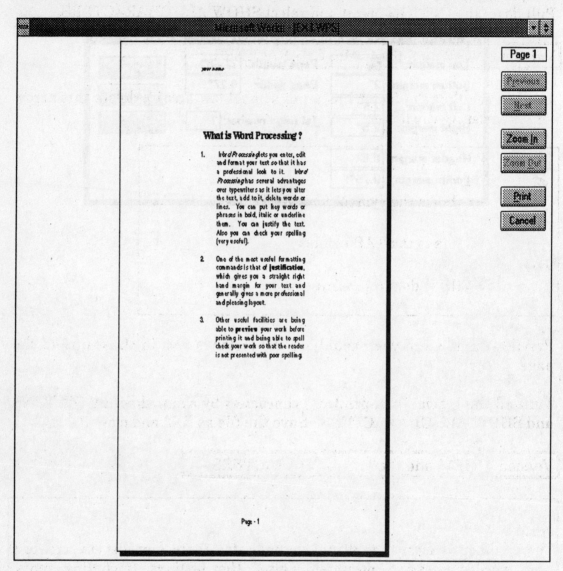

Notice how the page number is not centred; this is because it is actually tabbed not centred.

Displaying special (non-printing) characters
Pull down the OPTION menu and select SHOW ALL CHARACTERS.

> Version 3 VIEW and then ALL CHARACTERS.

You can see that the footer has a tab symbol (an arrow); delete this arrow and then centre the footer.

¶   this is the symbol for a RETURN

→   this is the TAB symbol

.....   these dots represent spaces.

Preview the file and you should see the footer is now in the centre of the page.

Turn off the special (non-printing) characters by again choosing OPTIONS and SHOW ALL CHARACTERS. Save the file as EX3 and close it.

> Version 3 VIEW and then ALL CHARACTERS.

Note :
To permanently alter the settings for page size, fonts, margins etc., create a new word processing document, alter the settings (including fonts, alignment and so on) and then select SAVE AS and alter the SAVE FILE AS TYPE box to WP TEMPLATE. You will be asked if you want to replace the existing file; answer YES and you have a new template.

In version 3 click on the TEMPLATES button to the right of the dialog box to create a new template.

Session 13: New features of version 3

Objectives

By the end of this session you will be able to:
Insert bullets automatically into your work.
Create a document containing columns
Use the text wrap feature for graphics
Insert tables into a document

Version 3 of the program contains some sophisticated features usually found only in more expensive programs. This session looks at the most useful.

Bullets

To begin you are going to practice your copying and pasting technique.

Create a new word processing document.

Open the file EX1.WPS and highlight the text. Use the toolbar buttons to COPY the text. Close the file EX1.WPS.

Use the toolbar button to PASTE the text into your new document and save the document as NEWORK.WPS.

Now copy the text once so that you have two copies of the same text (this is simply a mechanism to obtain a page of text without having to type it in, but also practices a useful technique).

Position the cursor at the beginning of the first paragraph and then click on the BULLETS button on the toolbar. You should now have an indented paragraph with a bullet.

Highlight the remainder of the text and then click on the bullets button again. All the paragraphs should now be bulleted and indented.

Columns

To produce a document divided into columns simply pull down the FORMAT menu and select COLUMNS. Enter the number 2 for the number of columns and make sure that the box for a LINE BETWEEN columns has a cross in it.

Then click on OK and you will see your document divided into two columns. You will be asked if you want to switch to PAGE LAYOUT view, this is sensible since it will let you edit the document in its columnar format.

Note:

Works will divide the whole document into columns, to have a document partly composed of columns will involve you in creating more than one file.

You can alter the page back to single column by the same method.

Text Wrap

Another useful feature is being able to wrap text around the pictures or other objects.

Position the cursor within a paragraph and pull down the INSERT menu and select CLIPART. From the list choose any picture and click on OK.

When it has been incorporated into the document, click on it and then FORMAT and PICTURE/OBJECT. Reduce its size to 50%.

From the FORMAT PICTURE dialog box choose TEXT WRAP and then click on ABSOLUTE and then click on OK. Finally click on the object within the document and drag it where you want it to be.

Inserting Tables

This involves making use of features found within the spreadsheet and is a useful way of laying out your text in tables which can be shaded for effect.

To begin position the cursor at the end of the second column and click on the INSERT TABLE button on the toolbar and then on OK.

A small table will appear (it looks like a miniature spreadsheet which is what it actually is).

Enter the following data.

Product	Cost	Number
Teddy bears	5.99	2
Gollies	4.49	5
Water rats	6.95	1

Highlight the second and third columns and select FORMAT and then ALIGNMENT so that the data is aligned to the RIGHT by clicking in the appropriate circle.

Again highlight the second and third columns and choose FORMAT but this time select COLUMN WIDTH and alter the column width of the second and third columns to BEST FIT by clicking in the BEST FIT box.

Highlight all the data and then select the FORMAT menu and choose BORDERS.

Click on outline and then on a thick line style.

Now highlight just the headings and again select PATTERNS. Choose a light shading. Finally click outside the table and you should see it within the document.

Centre the table and the final result should look like this.

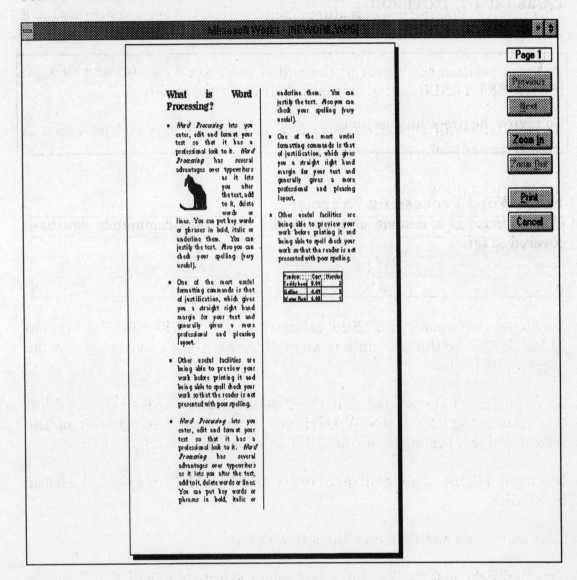

Finally print the file and save it before closing it.

Session 14: Revision

Objectives

To revise the preceding sections.

Final Word Processing Exercise
This exercise is a resume of some of the important commands you have covered so far.

Tasks

1.   Create a new word processing file.

2.   Enter the following text.

Discs
There are two types of computer disc, a hard disc which is used to store programs and data and a floppy disc which is used for back-ups and to store data files which can then be used on a different computer.

Floppy discs are so-called since they are made of a floppy plastic and are then held in rigid plastic or card. It is not a good idea to try to disassemble the case as you will not be able to put it back together again.

Almost all business computers use IBM compatible floppy discs and these are already formatted for use or may have to be formatted by you. If you need to format them then you will be told how to do this by your lecturer or by the computing staff.

Floppy discs come in two sizes, 5.25" and 3.5". Nowadays 3.5" discs are the standard as they are less fragile and can store rather more data than the older 5.25" floppy discs.

---

3.   Spell check your work and then read it through as spell checking will not pick up certain errors (e.g. grammar or the use of a word which is spelt correctly but is not the right word).

4.   Format the title to bold and put it in a font four points larger than the rest of the text, then centre it.

5.   Enter a blank line between the title and the remainder of the text.

6.   Justify the text (but not the heading).

7.   Number the first two paragraphs and indent them by using the hanging indent command.

8.   Swap the third and fourth paragraphs around.

9.   Indent the fourth paragraph by 1" left and 1" right.

10.   Double space the third paragraph.

11.   Put a normal border around the second paragraph.

12.   Create two more blank lines between the title and the text and then move the cursor into the middle of this space.

13.   Insert a picture into this space (DISK35.WMF) and then centre the picture. In version 3 choose a different image.

14.   Find and replace the word discs with the word DISKS (paying attention to the case)

15.   Add your name as a header and page numbers as the footer; format them both to italic and two points smaller than the rest of the text, then centre them.

16.   Alter both the left and right page margins to 1.5".

17.   Preview your work and, if successful, print it out.

18.   Save the file as **EX9** and close the file.

The finished result will look like this.

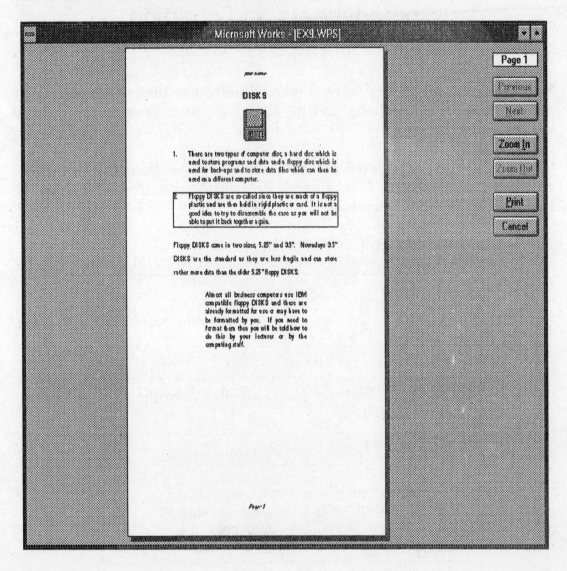

Spreadsheets and charting

Starting Off

Spreadsheets are used to solve financial and other numeric problems by automating the calculations and by allowing you to look at the data in various ways.

The actual program is based around cells made by a grid of rows (across) and columns (down). Text, figures or calculations (formulae) can be entered into any individual cell.

The typical layout of a spreadsheet is shown below:

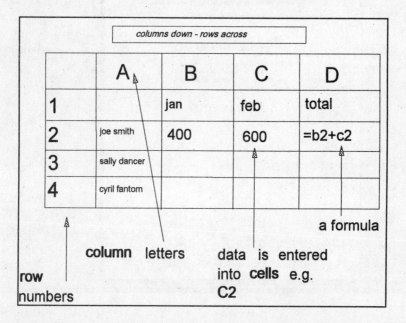

One of the attractions of spreadsheets is being able to use formulae for the calculations; having inserted formulae into cells any change to any of the figures in the cells will be automatically reflected in the answer (the program having been told how to calculate the answer, not what the answer is, so the answer is recalculated whenever the figures are changed).

Time can be saved by being able to copy not just text or numbers into other cells but also formulae, which can also reduce mistakes.

Another of the major benefits of using spreadsheets is being able to ask "What If" questions. For example, if you had created a worksheet for the next year's sales budgets you could then alter various figures to see what would happen in different situations. This would give you instant feedback and enable you to make more coherent and accurate decisions.

The reason why spreadsheets are so popular is that numbers are the mainstay of office work and spreadsheets are easy to use, and being able to have immediate feedback on any changes to the figures is very useful.

The spreadsheet and charting section contains the following sessions:

Starting Off
Session 15: Creating your first worksheet
Session 16: Formatting
Session 17: Exercise
Session 18: Sorting, borders and layout
Session 19: Exercise
Session 20: Charting
Session 21: Chart layout and types
Session 22: Copying charts
Session 23: Exercise
Session 24: Pie Charts
Session 25: Building up a chart
Session 26: A final spreadsheet and charting exercise

Session 15: Creating your first worksheet

Objectives

By the end of this session you will be able to :
Create a new spreadsheet file
Enter data
Enter a formula

Starting off

When you create a new spreadsheet file (FILE and then CREATE NEW
FILE or click on the spreadsheet icon in the startup screen), the following
screen will appear.

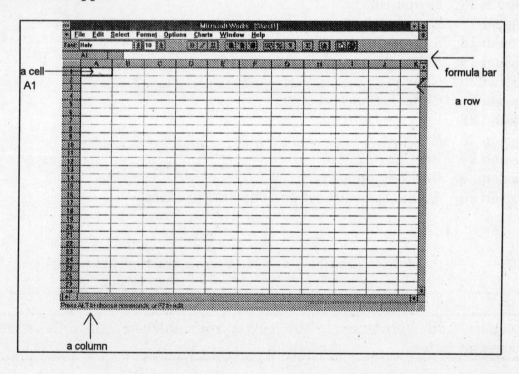

Much of the screen is similar to the word processing screen; the main differences are in the way the working area is divided into:

CELLS   each small box is called a cell and is identified by a cell reference e.g. **A1**.

ROWS   these go **across** the screen (and are numbered).

COLUMNS   these go **down** the screen (and named with a letter).

The toolbar is slightly different as well; the new buttons are identified below.

this formats the highlighted cells to currency

this formats the highlighted cells to a percentage

this introduces a comma into the highlighted cells

this adds up the cells

this button creates a new chart from the highlighted cells

In version 3 the differences in the toolbar are similar to that in the Word Processing section.

Entering data into the cells
You can enter either

TEXT or

NUMBERS or

FORMULAE

into a cell.

A formula is a mathematical expression explaining how to carry out a calculation.

To actually enter data click the cursor in a cell and then type in the relevant data. You will notice that the data is shown both in the cell and in the formula bar above.

After entering data into a specific cell, you can RETURN or just move the cursor to another cell by using either the cursor keys or the mouse (you must do one or the other).

To begin, create a new spreadsheet file and enter the data (shown below) into the cells.

See how if you enter jan into cell B1 it is automatically translated to January.

	A	B	C	D	E	F	G
1	Person	January	February	March	April	May	June
2	Rank.C	3000	1500	4300	3200	4400	5400
3	Poke.S	4000	2300	1200	6500	8800	7200
4	Earing.B	2000	3200	5400	2300	9800	8200
5	Rease.G	1000	1200	3200	6100	3200	10900
6	Lip.C	4000	5400	4500	7100	1200	7500

Note :
Dates and numbers align to the right of the cell and words align to the left.

Entering a formula

Now you are going to add up each of the columns. To do this simply click
the mouse in cell B7 and then click on the add symbol.

A formula to add up cells B2 to B6 will be shown in the cell B7 and in the
formula bar (above). The formula should show as

=SUM(B2:B6)

If it does then RETURN and the answer will be displayed in the cell.

Notes :
Always position the cursor in the cell you want the answer to appear in
before starting a formula.

Using the add button will add ALL the cells in the column or row, if you
only want to add some then you will have to enter the formula manually or
highlight the cells you want to include **after** clicking on the ADD button
and RETURN when finished

Please note that the **=** sign is **very** necessary as it means that you are
entering a formula.

One of the advantages of a spreadsheet is being able to copy words, numbers and formulae from one cell to another.

You are going to copy the formula in cell B7 across to cells C7 to G7.

To do this click the mouse on cell B7 and holding the mouse button down drag the mouse so that all the cells from B7 to G7 are highlighted.

Then pull down the EDIT menu and click on FILL RIGHT. This copies the formula into the cells (but the actual answer is displayed in the spreadsheet).

Now enter the word

```
Total
```

in cell A7.

The screen should now look like this.

	A	B	C	D	E	F	G
1	Person	January	February	March	April	May	June
2	Rank.C	3000	1500	4300	3200	4400	5400
3	Poke.S	4000	2300	1200	6500	8800	7200
4	Earing.B	2000	3200	5400	2300	9800	8200
5	Rease.G	1000	1200	3200	6100	3200	10900
6	Lip.C	4000	5400	4500	7100	1200	7500
7	Total	14000	13600	18600	25200	27400	39200

Enter the word

```
Total
```

in cell H1

Position the cursor in cell H2 and add up the cells in row 2 by using the add button.

Then use EDIT and FILL DOWN to copy the formula into cells H3 to H7.

Your screen should now look like this.

	A	B	C	D	E	F	G	H
1	Person	January	February	March	April	May	June	Total
2	Rank.C	3000	1500	4300	3200	4400	5400	21800
3	Poke.S	4000	2300	1200	6500	8800	7200	30000
4	Earing.B	2000	3200	5400	2300	9800	8200	30900
5	Rease.G	1000	1200	3200	6100	3200	10900	25600
6	Lip.C	4000	5400	4500	7100	1200	7500	29700
7	Total	14000	13600	18600	25200	27400	39200	138000

Save the file as EX10.

Session 16: Formatting

Objectives

By the end of the session you will be able to :
Format the cells
Enter more sophisticated formulae

Formatting the cells

So far you have accepted how the cells are formatted, now you will make the finished result look more professional.

Firstly click in cell H1 and then click on the right alignment button in the toolbar so that the word moves to the right and is aligned over the figures.

Note :
It is always better to align the text over the numbers rather than the other way around, since the numbers should be right aligned so that they line up underneath each other properly.

Highlight all the text in row 1 and format it to bold (using the bold button in the toolbar). Do the same for the words in column A.

Click the mouse in cell A1 and pull down the EDIT menu and then select INSERT ROW/COLUMN and choose ROW from the dialog box that appears.

In version 3 you should use the INSERT menu and then ROW/COLUMN.

A blank row should appear and all the other rows move down.

Enter the following into cell A1

Salespersons performance table

Format it to italic and bold and insert another blank line between the heading and the rest of the table.

It should look like this.

	A	B	C	D	E	F	G	H
1	*Salespersons performance table*							
2								
3	Person	January	February	March	April	May	June	Total
4	Rank.C	3000	1500	4300	3200	4400	5400	21800
5	Poke.S	4000	2300	1200	6500	8800	7200	30000
6	Earing.B	2000	3200	5400	2300	9800	8200	30900
7	Rease.G	1000	1200	3200	6100	3200	10900	25600
8	Lip.C	4000	5400	4500	7100	1200	7500	29700
9	Total	14000	13600	18600	25200	27400	39200	138000

Save the file (as EX10).

More on formulae

Now to enter a formula to calculate the average sales for each month.

Enter the word

```
Average
```

into cell A10.

Enter the following formula into cell B10.

```
=AVG(B4:B8)
```

The colon defines the range of cells being included in the calculation.

Fill this formula right from cell B10 to H10.

Finally format the whole row to bold and insert a blank line between the names and the total row and between the total and average rows. Your spreadsheet should look similar to this.

	A	B	C	D	E	F	G	H
1	Salespersons performance table							
2								
3	Person	January	February	March	April	May	June	Total
4	Rank.C	3000	1500	4300	3200	4400	5400	21800
5	Poke.S	4000	2300	1200	6500	8800	7200	30000
6	Earing.B	2000	3200	5400	2300	9800	8200	30900
7	Rease.G	1000	1200	3200	6100	3200	10900	25600
8	Lip.C	4000	5400	4500	7100	1200	7500	29700
9								
10	Total	14000	13600	18600	25200	27400	39200	138000
11								
12	Average	2800	2720	3720	5040	5480	7840	27600

Save the file as EX10 and close the file.

Session 17: Exercise

Objectives

To revise the work covered so far

Tasks
Create a new spreadsheet file.

Enter the following data.

	A	B	C	D
1		Hours	Pay rate	Gross pay
2	Ox.B	35	3.45	
3	Ace.L	21	5.32	
4	Andle.H	56	6.32	
5	Able.T	40	3.65	

Notes :
Remember that when creating a formula to make sure that you have clicked the mouse in the cell you want the answer to appear in **before** starting the process.

All formulae must begin with an = sign.

Calculate the gross pay by entering a formula in cell D2 (hours $*$ pay rate), the multiplication symbol is a star.

The formula should be :

```
=B2*C2
```

Then FILL DOWN into the other cells

Note :
You do not need to use a function like SUM or AVG for multiplication, division or subtraction, **only the calculation e.g. =D7*E2 followed by** RETURN.

Enter the word

```
Total
```

into cell A6.

Sum (add up) the total gross pay.

Format the headings to bold.

Your screen should now look like this.

	A	Hours	Pay rate	Gross pay
1		Hours	Pay rate	Gross pay
2	Ox.B	35	3.45	120.75
3	Ace.L	21	5.32	111.72
4	Andle.H	56	6.32	353.92
5	Able.T	40	3.65	146
6	Total			732.39

Save the file as EX11 and close it.

Session 18: Sorting, borders and layout

Objectives

By the end of this session you will be able to :
Sort data
Place a border around data
Insert headers and footers
Set margins
Print a spreadsheet

More on formatting cells

There are several very useful commands which enable you to lay out your spreadsheet in the best possible way.

For example, you can add commas to the figures or you can define how many decimal places to allocate to any of the cells.

Open the file EX10 and highlight all the cells containing numbers.

Pull down the FORMAT menu and select COMMA. You will be asked for the number of decimal places you want (the default is 2).

In version 3, select FORMAT then NUMBER and finally COMMA.

Accept the default of 2 decimal places and click on OK.

The figures will now be formatted with commas and two decimal places.

Other useful number formats are.

General	Best fit, this is the way numbers are formatted by default.
Fixed	You can choose how many decimal places you want to have for the highlighted figures.
Currency	With pounds signs and a choice of decimal places.
Comma	Commas with a choice of decimal places.
Percent	Shows the figures as a percentage.

Sorting the data

You may want to sort the data in various ways.

Using EX10 you are going to sort the names into alphabetical order

Highlight the cells A4 to H8 and then pull down the SELECT menu and choose SORT ROWS.

In version 3 the commands are TOOLS and then SORT ROWS.

You will see the following dialog box appear.

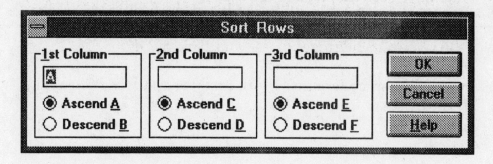

You can choose up to three columns to include in the sort, the first being the primary field and so on.

In this example, enter **A** into the 1st Column box and then click on OK.

The names will have been sorted into alphabetic order.

The result should look like this.

	A	B	C	D	E	F	G	H
1	Salespersons performance table							
2								
3	Person	January	February	March	April	May	June	Total
4	Earing.B	2,000.00	3,200.00	5,400.00	2,300.00	9,800.00	8,200.00	30,900.00
5	Lip.C	4,000.00	5,400.00	4,500.00	7,100.00	1,200.00	7,500.00	29,700.00
6	Poke.S	4,000.00	2,300.00	1,200.00	6,500.00	8,800.00	7,200.00	30,000.00
7	Rank.C	3,000.00	1,500.00	4,300.00	3,200.00	4,400.00	5,400.00	21,800.00
8	Rease.G	1,000.00	1,200.00	3,200.00	6,100.00	3,200.00	10,900.00	25,600.00
9								
10	Total	14,000.00	13,600.00	18,600.00	25,200.00	27,400.00	39,200.00	138,000.00
11								
12	Average	2,800.00	2,720.00	3,720.00	5,040.00	5,480.00	7,840.00	27,600.00

See how the rest of the data will have been moved with the names so that the figures for each name are the same as they were before the sort.

Note :
Be careful when sorting to only highlight the data you actually want to sort.   For example, if you had included the titles when highlighting then they would have been included in the sort.

Cell borders

You can place borders around your work to make it look more professional. This is very similar to the borders command within the word processing module although you have only one type of border available.

To do this highlight all your work and then pull down the FORMAT menu and select BORDER command, then click on OUTLINE so that an X appears in the box and then click on OK.

Version 3 lets you choose different line styles and you can apply shading by choosing FORMAT and then PATTERNS.

You will be able to see the border better when you preview the file. Do not worry if the right hand border does not appear (you will correct this later).

Headers and footers

Just like in the word processing module you can add page numbers and headers to your work.

Pull down the EDIT menu and then HEADERS & FOOTERS and you will see the dialog box.

In version 3 select the VIEW menu and then HEADERS & FOOTERS.

Headers & Footers

Header: [   ]   OK
Footer: [   ]   Cancel

☐ No header on 1st page   ☐ Use header and   Help
☐ No footer on 1st page   footer paragraphs

Note that you cannot just click on USE HEADER AND FOOTER PARAGRAPHS but have to enter the text within the boxes (as you could have done within the word processing module if you had wished).

Enter a header of your name.

Enter the following into the footer box (this puts a page number centred on the page),

page &c&p

and then click on OK.

Other codes are

&d   the date
&n   the date in longer format
&t   the time
&l   align left
&r   align right

these can be combined as you wish and can be used in the word processing and database modules as well.

You will not see these on the page but will be able to see them when you preview the file.

Save the file as EX10.

Margins

You can alter the margins in the same way as you did with the word processing files (FILE and then PAGE SETUP & MARGINS) if necessary.

Try this by altering the left and right margins to 2" each (again you will not see the change until you print preview the file).

Version 3 the commands are FILE, then PAGE SETUP and finally MARGINS.

Save the file as EX10.

Printing out

Preview the file EX10 and you will see that it does not fit onto one page.

This is a problem and there are several things you can do to avoid this.

---
1. Alter the font to a smaller size (you may want to change the font as well as some look better than others). Unfortunately, unlike the word processor, altering the font affects the whole of the spreadsheet.

2. Change the margins of the page so that they are as narrow as possible.

3. Alter the column widths.

4. Change the page orientation to landscape (rather than portrait).

You are going to try each of these in turn.

Font size
Choose a font size two points smaller than the original and then preview the file to see if it will fit on one page. Make the font size smaller until it does fit.

Change the font size back to the original size.

Margins
Alter the left and right margins to 0.5" each. Preview the file and if it does not fit keep making them smaller until it fits on one page.

Alter the margins back to 1.25" each.

Column width
Highlight all the columns and then pull down the FORMAT menu and select COLUMN WIDTH. Enter the figure

9

and click on OK.

This will alter the widths of all the highlighted columns to 9 (characters) and you will see the following symbols in the last column.

######

When you see this symbol in a spreadsheet it means that the column is not wide enough for the figures being displayed; the answer is simply to widen the column.

Position the cursor in column H and pull down the FORMAT menu and select COLUMN WIDTH and enter the figure.

10

When you preview the file it should fit on one page.

Notes :
You can also alter the column width using the mouse. To do so, position the mouse within the column bar at the junction between two columns and the cursor will change to a two-headed cross. You can then click and drag this to the new position.

Version 3 lets you alter the width of each row by the same technique.

If one of these methods does not work on its own, you may have to combine them to achieve the desired result.

Page orientation
To change to landscape pull down the FILE menu and select PAGE SETUP & MARGINS.

Swop the length and width measurements around (with A4 paper this means that the length will be 8.27" and the width 11.69").

Version 3 the sequence is PAGE SETUP, SOURCE AND ORIENTATION and then click on LANDSCAPE

Then pull down the FILE menu again and select PRINTER SETUP.

You will see a similar dialog box to that shown below (version 3 you may need to choose SETUP within the initial dialog box)

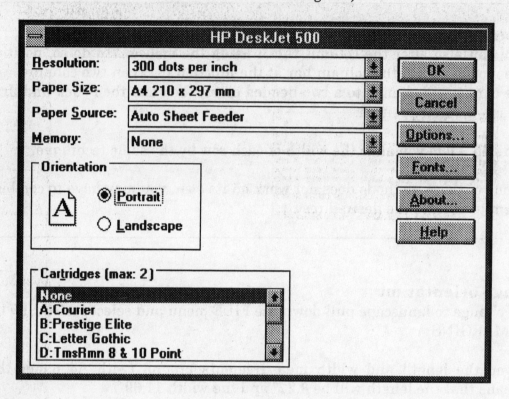

Alter the orientation by clicking on Landscape and then on OK.

Preview the file and it should now look like that shown below.

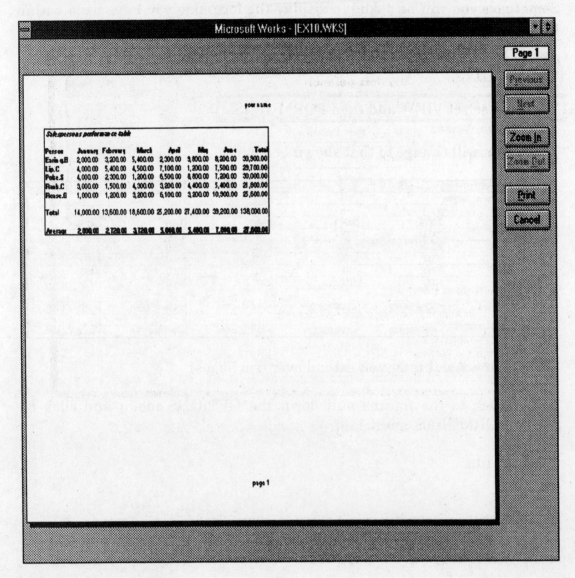

Save the file as EX10.

Displaying the formulae

Sometimes you will be asked to display the formulae you have used within the spreadsheet.

To do this pull down the OPTIONS menu and click on SHOW FORMULAS.

Version 3 select VIEW and then FORMULAS.

The screen will change to that shown below.

	A	B	C	D	E	F
1	Salespersons perfor					
2						
3	Person	33970	34001	34029	34060	34090
4	Earing.B	2000	3200	5400	2300	9800
5	Lip.C	4000	5400	4500	7100	1200
6	Poke.S	4000	2300	1200	6500	8800
7	Rank.C	3000	1500	4300	3200	4400
8	Rease.G	1000	1200	3200	6100	3200
9						
10	Total	=SUM(B4:B8)	=SUM(C4:C8)	=SUM(D4:D8)	=SUM(E4:E8)	=SUM(F4:F8)
11						
12	Average	=AVG(B4:B8)	=AVG(C4:C8)	=AVG(D4:D8)	=AVG(E4:E8)	=AVG(F4:F8)

You can preview this (it will extend over two pages).

To get back to the figures pull down the OPTIONS menu and click on SHOW FORMULAS again.

Close the file.

Session 19: Exercise

Objectives

To revise the previous sections.

Tasks

1.   Create a new spreadsheet file.

2.   Enter the following data.

Hints.
- you will need to alter the width of some of the columns.
- after entering the word January, highlight the cells for the rest of the months and then click on EDIT and FILL SERIES and MONTH.

Fiona's Food Ltd							
Profit and loss for jan 1993 to july 1993							
	January	February	March	April	May	June	July
Sales of food	200	250	290	310	340	220	450
Tips	30	43	54	32	26	21	67
Total income							
Wages	60	60	60	60	60	60	60
Food purchases	60	75	87	93	102	66	135
Heat	20	25	29	31	34	22	45
Rent	30	30	30	30	30	30	30
Rates	100						
Motor expenses	43	47	54	43	65	59	62
Total Expenses							
Net Income							

3.	Enter formulae into the remaining cells, i.e. total income, total expenses and net income. (Remember to use SUM or the sum button in the toolbar to add up, and FILL RIGHT to copy the formula across)

4.	Format the headings (including the months) to bold.

5.	Sort the expenses into alphabetical order.

6.	Format the figures to currency (no decimal places).

7.	Enter your name as a header and the date as the footer (both centred).

8.	Place a border around the spreadsheet.

9.	Change the orientation to landscape and preview the file.

It should look like this.

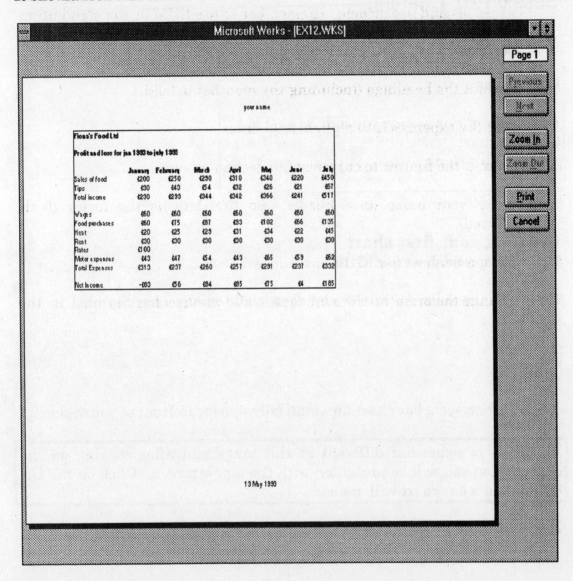

10.   If successful print it out, save the file as EX12 and close it.

Session 20: Charting

Objectives

By the end of this session you will be able to :
Create a chart
Add text to a chart

Creating your first chart
Open the spreadsheet file EX10.

Highlight the cells A3 to G8 and then click on the chart symbol in the toolbar.

You will then see a bar chart automatically appear in front of your eyes !.

Version 3 is somewhat different at this stage and after clicking on the chart button you will be presented with the a new screen. Click on the OK button and a bar chart will appear.

The screen should look like this.

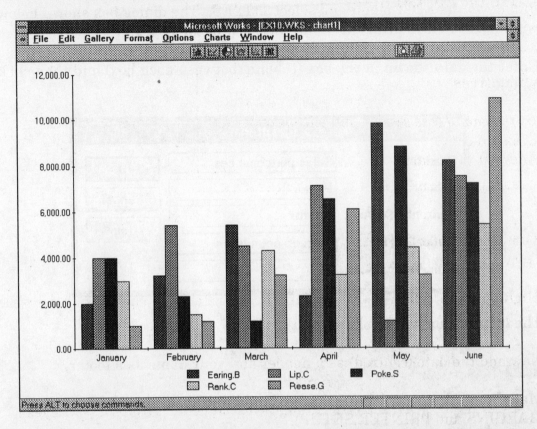

You are now in the charting part of the program and can alter the chart to another type of chart, e.g. a line graph or pie chart and so on, and you can make the chart more meaningful by adding text and other useful effects.

Adding text to the chart

You create a chart so that you can communicate numeric data more effectively to the reader. Any additional information you can provide will make communication more effective.

Adding a title

Pull down the EDIT menu and select TITLES. The dialog box shown below will appear and you can enter data into any of the boxes.

Enter the data shown in the box (tabbing between each box) and then click on OK.

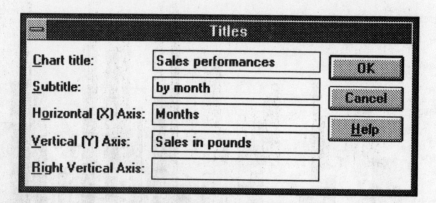

The information will be shown on the chart.

Now add the date (centred) as a header and your name as a footer.

Make sure that you have selected landscape (both in PAGE SETUP & MARGINS and PRINTER SETUP).

Preview your work, it should look like this.

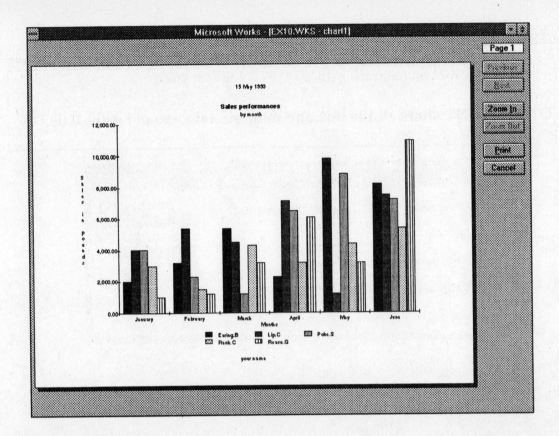

Changing fonts

You can alter the look of the text by changing the font, its size or by formatting the characters to bold, italic or underlined.

Pull down the FORMAT menu and select TITLE FONT. Choose ARIAL 16 point bold and then click on OK.

> In version 3 you will need to highlight the title by clicking on it and then selecting FORMAT followed by FONT & STYLE. Likewise with other fonts only this time you do not have to highlight them.

Do the same for the OTHER FONT, this time choosing ARIAL 12 point (not bold). You can now see how changing the fonts alters the look of the chart.

Save the file as EX10 and close the files.

Note :
OTHER FONT alters all the text and numeric data except for the title.

Session 21: Chart layout and types

Objectives

By the end of this session you will be able to :
Add gridlines to the chart
Alter the patterns
Place a border around the chart
Alter the type of chart

Adding gridlines

Open the file EX10 and display your chart on screen by pulling down the
CHARTS menu and selecting CHART1.

In version 3 select VIEW and then CHART.

If necessary enlarge the chart to full screen by clicking on the up arrow in
the top right of the chart window.

You are going to add gridlines to your chart.

Gridlines can be either horizontal or vertical and help the reader to see the
values being charted.

To add horizontal gridlines pull down the FORMAT menu and select
VERTICAL (Y) AXIS. You will see a dialog box appear (see next page).
Click on SHOW GRIDLINES so that an **X** appears in the box, then click on
OK and horizontal gridlines will be shown on your chart.

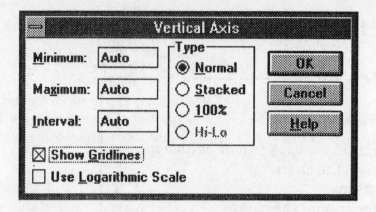

Showing the chart in black and white.

Unless you are using a colour printer it is better to view the chart as it will appear on the printed page.

To do this pull down the OPTIONS menu and select DISPLAY AS PRINTED, the chart will now appear in black and white.

> Version 3 select the VIEW menu instead of the OPTIONS menu.

Changing the patterns for the chart

The default colours and shading can be altered. Often they will look better in black and white printing if you make them less dense.

To change them, pull down the FORMAT menu and select PATTERNS & COLORS. A dialog box will appear.

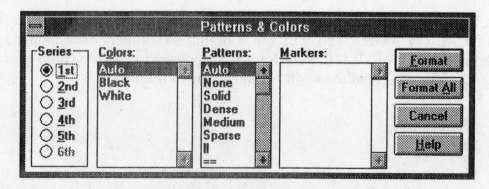

Each different coloured bar represents a different series (in your chart you have five different series).

To alter each, select the series number you want to alter, then the colour and then the pattern you want (with certain types of chart, for example a line chart, you will also be able to change the markers on each line). After altering each series click on FORMAT and then alter the next series, and so on.

Note :
With some of the boxes (e.g. PATTERNS) there are arrows to the right of the box, this means that there are further items not displayed. You can scroll the display (move it up and down) by clicking on the arrows.

Look at the example (on the next page) to see the effect of changing the colours and patterns of the bars.

Placing a border around your chart

Often your chart will look more attractive with a border around it. To do this choose FORMAT and then SHOW BORDER.

In version 3 select FORMAT and then ADD BORDER.

Your chart should now look similar to this.

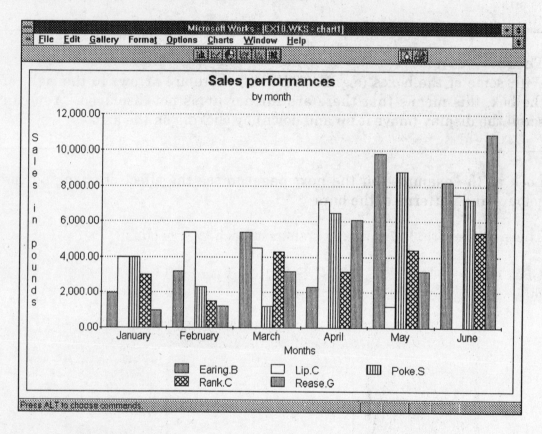

Choosing the chart type

When you start charting you will always get a bar chart and in many situations this is the best chart to display information.

WORKS lets you alter this by clicking on any of the alternative chart buttons in the toolbar (shown below).

The charts available are (in order)

BAR CHARTS
LINE CHARTS
PIE CHARTS (dealt with separately later)
STACKED LINE CHARTS
XY (SCATTER) CHARTS
COMBINATION CHARTS

There are several alternative versions of each type of chart.

Click on the button for LINE CHARTS and you will be presented with the following choice of different line graphs.

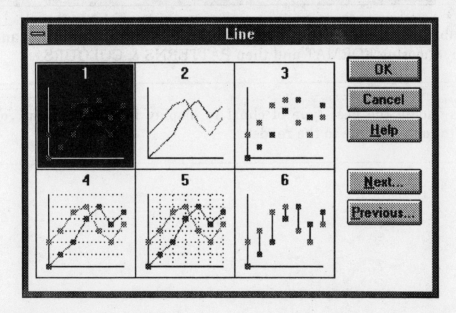

Click on choice number 5 (which already includes both X and Y axis gridlines) and then on OK and you should see the following appear.

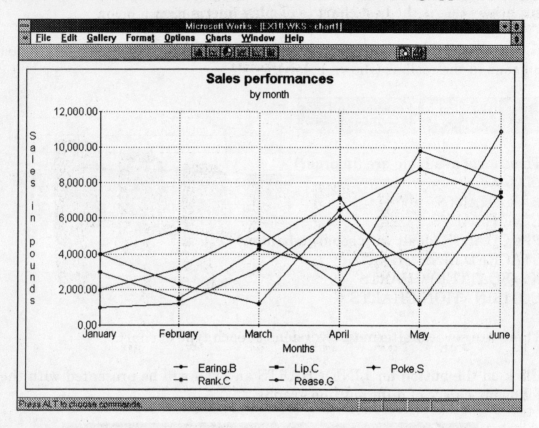

Remember, if the lines and markers look too similar then you can alter them by choosing FORMAT and then PATTERNS & COLOURS.

Always choose the best type of chart to display the information you are trying to communicate to the reader.

Version 3 has a larger choice of chart types as you can see from the toolbar, you can choose 3-D charts which can be very effective, although you should use them with care. An example of a 3-D chart is shown below.

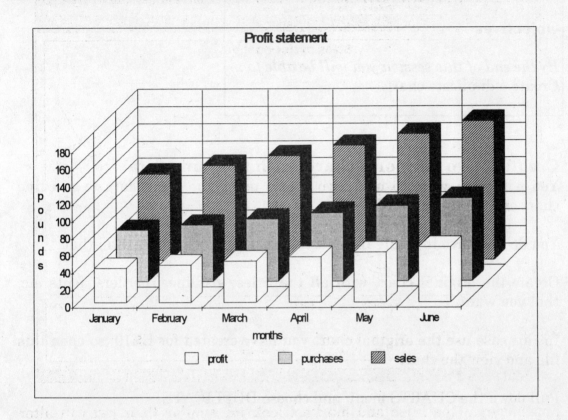

Returning to the spreadsheet

Click on the command WINDOW and then select the worksheet you want (or use the CTRL and F6 keys to switch back to the spreadsheet).

Save the file and close it.

Session 22: Copying charts

Objectives

By the end of this session you will be able to :
Create a duplicate chart

Creating two (or more) charts with the same data
You will often want to have two charts using the same data (e.g. a line chart and a bar chart).

You do **not** have to create the chart twice; it is much easier than that.

Create the original chart with all the titles, gridlines, borders, fonts etc. that you want.

In this case use the original chart you have created for EX10, so open this file and view the chart

Pull down the CHARTS menu and choose DUPLICATE.

In version 3 choose TOOLS and DUPLICATE CHART.

You will see a dialog box.

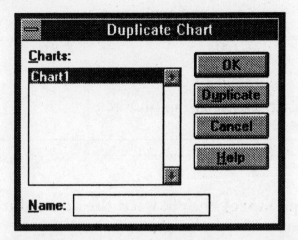

Enter the name you want to give the second chart by clicking in the NAME BOX and typing in the name (in this case CHART 2) and then click on DUPLICATE. The new name should appear below the original. If this works then click on OK and you have two identical charts.

Now simply pull down the CHARTS command and select the second chart. Click on the chart type you want from the toolbar (in this case choose a bar chart (No.4)) and you now have two different types of chart with the same data and formatting.

In version 3 choose VIEW and then CHART.

Note :
You can change the name of any chart or delete a chart by using the OPTIONS menu in a very similar way to duplicating a chart.

In version 3 the TOOLS menu is used instead of the OPTIONS menu.

Save and close all the files.

Session 23: Exercise

Objectives

To revise the preceding work on charts.

Tasks

Open the file EX11.

Create a bar chart using the data in the cells A1 to D5.

Add suitable titles and subtitles to the chart and the axes (include your name as the subtitle).

Alter the title and other fonts to give the best result.

Add horizontal gridlines to the chart.

Show the chart in black and white and alter the patterns as necessary.

Place a border around the chart.

Alter the page and printer setup to landscape and preview the file; it should look similar to this.

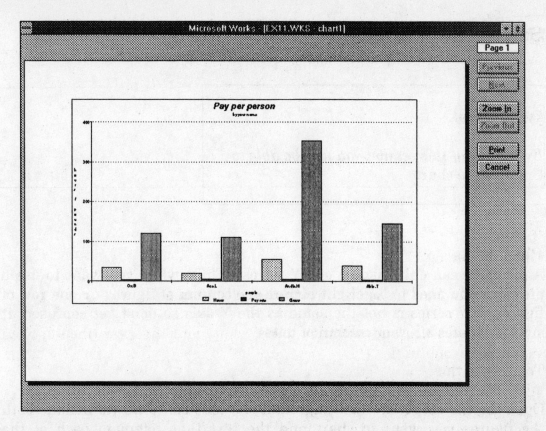

Save the file as EX11 and close it.

Session 24: Pie Charts

Objectives

By the end of this session you will be able to :
Create a pie chart

Pie Charts

A pie chart can only display one Y series. Thus, when you want to use a pie chart you need to highlight **either** one column of figures **or** one row of figures (a Y series is not the same as the Y axis so don't get confused, it simply denotes a row or column of data).

To practice this

Open the file EX11 and then highlight the cells A2 to B5 (to include both the figures you want to chart and the text that refers to each of the figures).

If using version 3 just accept the defaults on the initial chart dialog box.

Click on the chart button in the toolbar and after the default bar chart appears click on the PIE CHART button.

You will be given the following choices.

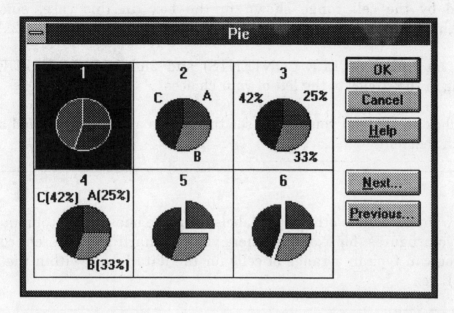

Accept choice 1 by clicking on OK and the chart will change to a pie.

Unfortunately this is pretty uninformative as there is no explanation of the information displayed. To add text pull down the EDIT menu and select DATA LABELS.

This lets you add detail to each of the segments in the pie (see below).

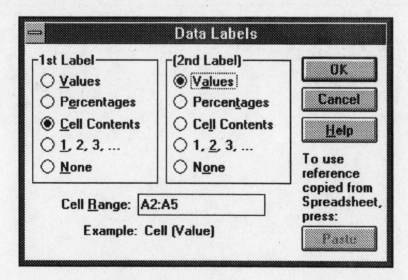

You can add two different labels to each segment, the actual detail being defined by the cell range shown in the box (in this case, since you highlighted the column to the left of the figures, the cell range is A2:A5)

Select 1st LABEL (CELL CONTENTS) and 2nd LABEL (VALUES) by clicking in the circles to the left of your choices.

Then click on OK and you should see the names and hours worked appear for each segment.

Note :
If you want to include other data labels than the ones in the column to the left of your figures (for example where you are charting a different column) then you can type in a range of cells for the data labels within the CELL RANGE box.

Now add a title and subtitle to your pie chart and change the colour of the slices (segments) of the pie in the same way you did for the bar chart.

The result may look similar to that shown below.

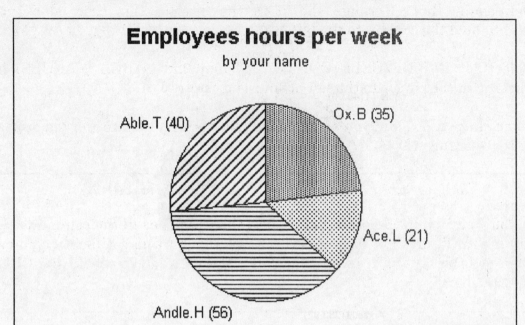

Save the file as EX11.

More on Pie Charts
You are going to create another pie chart for EX11, this time using the gross pay for each person. Format all the figures to 2 decimal places.

Create a bar chart for the gross pay for the people (D2:D5). Choose pie chart 6.

Add the names etc. by using EDIT and DATA LABELS and entering the range of cells you want to use for the labels in the CELL RANGE box (A2:A5) and then select cell contents for the 1st label and values for the 2nd label. The labels are shown in order on the pie chart.

Now add titles and alter the patterns as necessary. Put a border around the chart and preview it.

The result should be something like this.

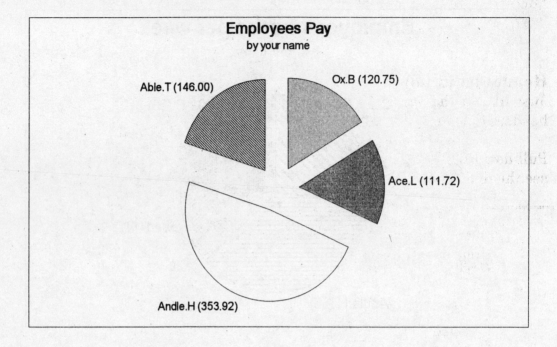

Employees Pay
by your name

Ox.B (120.75)

Able.T (146.00)

Ace.L (111.72)

Andle.H (353.92)

Save the file and close the files.

Session 25: Building up a chart

Objectives

By the end of this session you will be able to :
Build up a chart from parts of the spreadsheet

Building up a chart from its component values

Sometimes you may not be able to merely highlight the cells you want to
chart. It may be that the figures you want to chart do not lie in adjacent
columns.

To build up the chart is easy if you approach it sensibly.

Open up EX12 which you are going to use as a example.

Highlight **only** the figures in the Total Income row and click on the chart
button in the toolbar.

A bar chart will be displayed for this data.

Adding series

To add series simply pull down the EDIT menu and choose SERIES. The dialog box will be shown.

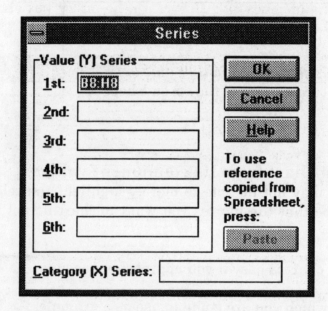

See how the first series you charted is shown. All you need to do is to type in the cell ranges for each series you want to include in the chart (it is worthwhile writing these down otherwise you will be continually switching backwards and forwards between the chart and worksheet).

You want to include two more rows, that of TOTAL EXPENSES (B16:H16) and that of NET INCOME (B18:H18). So enter each of these into the boxes for the 2nd and 3rd Y series.

Also enter the cell range for the months (B5:H5) into the CATEGORY X SERIES box so that they are displayed along the X axis. Then click on OK.

Adding legends

Now you need to add the legend for each series (a legend is a description of what each coloured bar or line in the chart represents), to do this pull down the EDIT menu and choose LEGEND. In the dialog box enter the cell you want to have as the legend for each series (shown below).

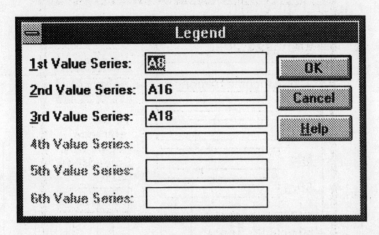

In version 3 you should remove the **X** from the AUTO SERIES LABELS box.

Other tasks (a little revision)

Add a suitable title and subtitle and titles for the X and Y axes.

Alter the colour and shading of the bars.

Place a border around the chart.

The result will look similar to this.

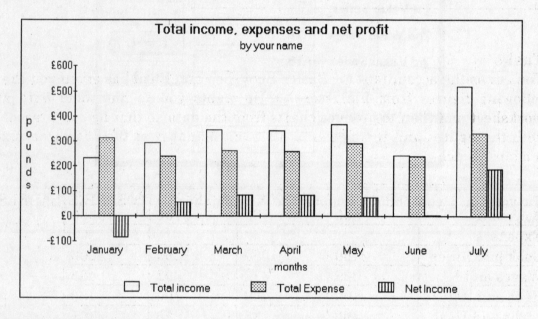

Now read through this section again paying particular attention to how the ranges were entered and how they appeared in the chart.

Save the file as EX12 and close it.

Session 26: A final spreadsheet and charting exercise

Objectives

To revise what you have learnt about charting.

Tasks

You act as the accountant for Basil's Bookshop and Basil has given you the following figures from his records. He wants you to put them onto a worksheet and then to produce charts from the data so that he can present both the figures and the charts to his bank manager at their forthcoming business lunch.

	Jan-Mar	Apr-Jun	Jul-Sept	Oct-Dec
Booksales	3800	4300	6700	9800
Expenses				
Book purchases	2100	1980	3200	4200
Wages and NI	309	312	302	465
Rent and Rates	100	100	100	100
Light and Heat	90	88	75	101

Spreadsheet

1. Enter these figures into a worksheet.

2. SUM the expenses for each period (remember to FILL RIGHT) and enter a heading for the row.

3. Total the figures for the whole year (title this column Totals).

4. Enter a formula to work out the profit for each period (booksales less total expenses).

5. Insert an additional column between Oct-Dec and the yearly totals, and give this the heading AVERAGES.

6. In this new column calculate the averages for each row for the four periods.

7. Format the column headings to bold.

8. Align the heading in the columns with figures to right alignment.

9. Format all the numbers to show commas but no decimal places.

10. Insert blank rows before the expenses, total expenses and profit.

11. Sort the expenses into alphabetical order.

12. Enter your name as a header and the date as a footer (centred).

13. Place a border around the figures.

14. Alter the column widths as necessary.

15. Preview the worksheet and print it out in landscape.

The worksheet should now look like this.

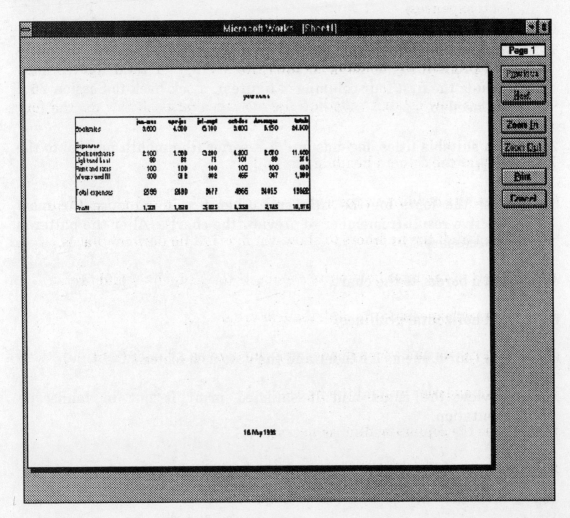

Save as EX13.

Charting

Chart 1

1. Create a bar chart from the data for the book sales, total expenses and profit rows (do NOT include the average or total figures, only include the first four columns of figures). Look back to Session 25 if you need to.

2. Add suitable titles, legends and a X-series (the month names) to the chart.

3. Alter the fonts for the title and other text to produce the most effective result (remember to preview the chart). Alter the patterns as necessary.

4. Add a border to the chart.

5. Add horizontal gridlines.

6. Add your name as a header and the date as a footer.

7. Preview the chart and if satisfied print it out in landscape orientation.

The first chart should look something like this.

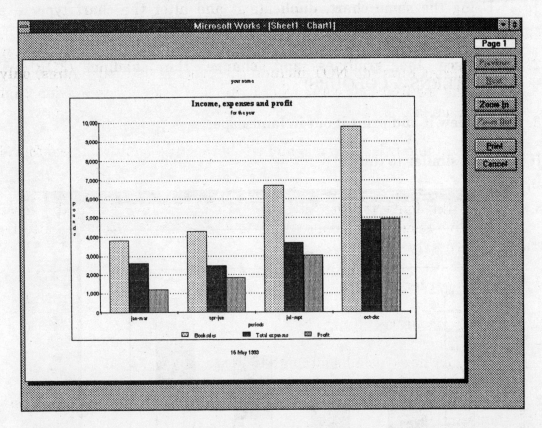

Chart 2

1. Using the same chart, duplicate it and alter the chart type to a stacked bar chart.

2. Replace the gridlines and change the shading (FORMAT PATTERNS & COLOURS).

3. Preview it and print it out in landscape.

It may look similar to this.

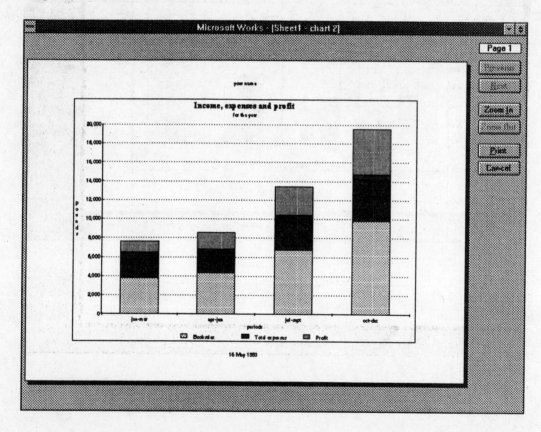

Chart 3

1. Duplicate it again and this time choose a line graph with gridlines.

2. Change the lines and markers so that they each look different (FORMAT PATTERNS & COLOURS).

3. Preview it and print it out in landscape (as shown below).

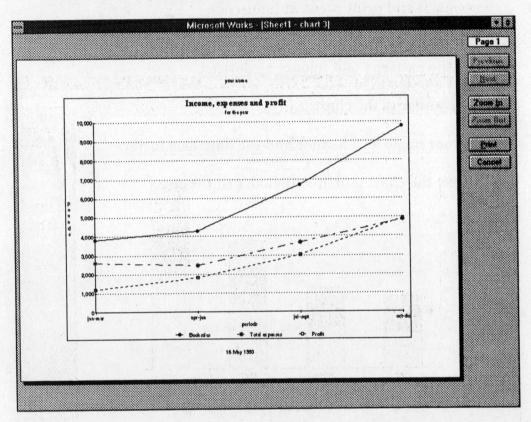

Chart 4

1. Produce an exploded pie chart from the book sales for each period (not the average or totals).

2. Add suitable labels to each slice of the pie.

3. Add suitable titles to the chart.

4. Alter the fonts for the title and other fonts as required.

5. Alter the patterns and colours as desired.

5. Add a border to the chart.

6. Add your name as a header and the date as a footer.

7. Preview the chart and, if satisfied, print it out.

It may look similar to that shown below.

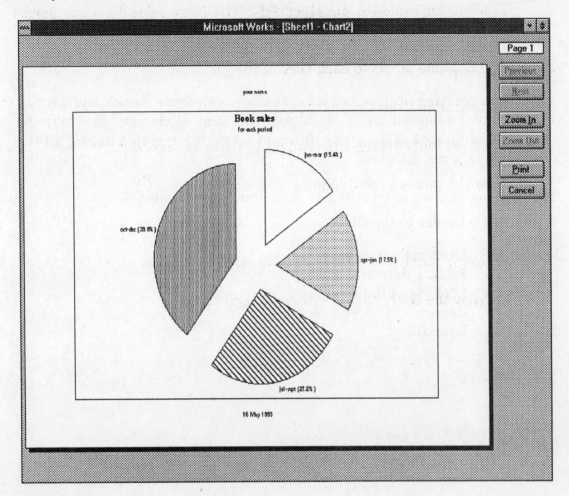

Save the file as EX13 and close it.

Databases

Starting Off

Databases are used to store facts, for example employee names and details. These may be stored in a database file and then the file may be interrogated (looked at) in many different ways, for example listing all the employees in a certain area.

The sections on databases contains the following sessions:

Starting Off
Session 27: Creating a database file
Session 28: Adding data and sorting
Session 29: Looking at the data
Session 30: Reports
Session 31: Exercise

What is a datafile

A datafile is made up of records. Each record contains data relating to a specific item, e.g. a person (similar to a record card in a card index).

A typical record card is shown below.

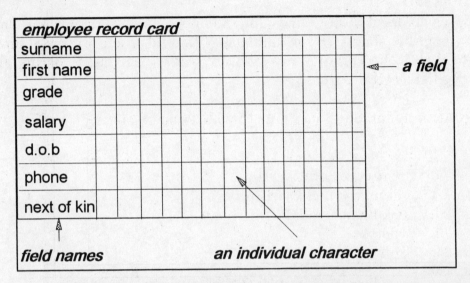

The initial screen that you will see when creating a new database file is shown on the next page. It is effectively a blank sheet for you to create a data entry screen.

| If you are using version 3 just click on the OK button on the initial dialog box if it appears. |

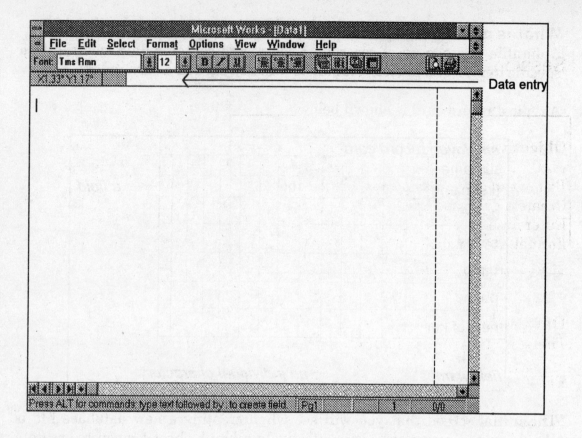

Data entry

New buttons

Shown below are the new buttons on the toolbar that are specific to the database.

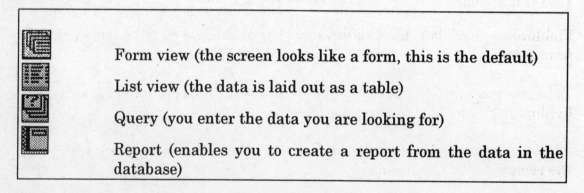

Form view (the screen looks like a form, this is the default)

List view (the data is laid out as a table)

Query (you enter the data you are looking for)

Report (enables you to create a report from the data in the database)

Each of these will be dealt with in turn.

Session 27: Creating a database file

Objectives

By the end of the session you will be able to :
Create a database form
Enter data in it
Format the layout

Data entry

There are two types of information you can type onto this screen.

TEXT or

FIELDNAMES

Text means any explanatory text you want to appear on the screen so that the person entering the information is given some help.

Text is entered as you want it to appear.

Fieldnames, however, have to have a colon at the end (to distinguish them from text).

To begin, you position the cursor where you want to begin entering either a fieldname or text and start typing.

As you can see from the screen on page 141 the first two lines are text and the remainder are fieldnames.

> **Note :**
> When you want to move either text or fieldnames then click the cursor on them (a little hand should appear) and drag them to a new position.
>
> In version 3 the word DRAG appears when you try to move anything.

When entering fieldnames you will be presented with a dialog box that asks for the width and height of the field (at this stage just accept the default as shown below).

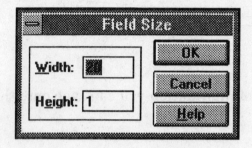

Create a data entry screen that looks similar to that shown below.

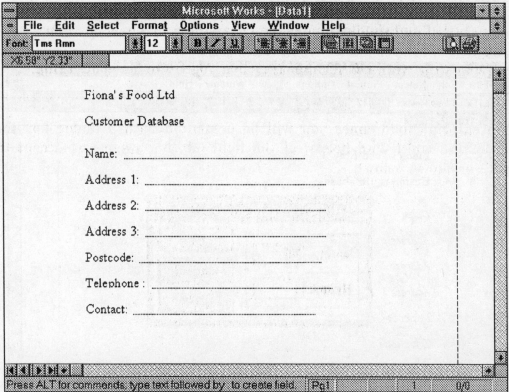

Formatting a form
See how the colons at the end of each fieldname are not lined up underneath each other.

To alter this simply click on each field in turn and then click in the data entry box.

You can then add spaces **before** the colon for each fieldname so that the colons for each field are lined up. To do this move the cursor (in the data entry box) just before the colon by using the cursor keys and then press the spacebar as many times as necessary. Hit the **RETURN key** when finished.

I suggest that you begin at the bottom and work up.

Now format the headings to bold and the field names to italic by clicking on each and then clicking the appropriate button on the toolbar.

The end result will look similar to this.

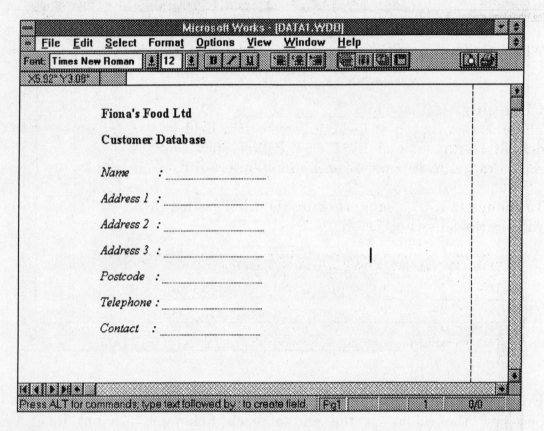

Enter the data shown below, you will need to increase the width of the NAME field to 28 characters wide by clicking on the field itself (not the field name) and then pulling down the FORMAT menu and selecting FIELD SIZE.

Entering the data

Having created the form you now need to actually enter the data. Position the cursor on the line to the right of the fieldname.

Enter the data (shown on the next page) one field at a time, tabbing onto the next field. Also use the TAB key to move onto the next record.

NAME	ADDRESS1	ADDRESS2	ADDRESS3	POSTCODE	TELEPHONE	CONTACT
Aunties Apple Pies PLC	The Old Farmhouse	Farnborough	Hants	AN56 6RE	0876-218934	Harriet Hammings
Kitchen Kapers Ltd	31 Crossways	Cambridge	Cambs	CA21 9UT	0564-125421	Mary Mattins
Foreign Foods	56 Arcade Crescent	Islington	London	IS8 56XT	081-435-8976	Ms. Frankhurt
Healthy Habits	Hort Court	Avimore	Scotland	GL23 9OU	0678-83256	Elisa Ellis
Useful Utensils	The Warren	Sea View	Weymouth	DO6 87R	0228-65743	Harrry Hannibal
The Fresh Fruit Co.	65 Currant Grove	Oxelhome	Cumbria	OX7 8TR	0338-111111	Samuel Spade
The Wholefood Warehouse	Warren Street	Exeter	Devon	EX98 5ED	0387-883311	Herbert Hedgehog

When you have finished entering **all** the data press RETURN.

Changing to list view

There are two ways of looking at the data held in a database file - the default FORM view or LIST view (which shows all the fields across the screen rather than showing each individual record one at a time).

To change to LIST simply click on the LIST button in the toolbar and you will see the following screen.

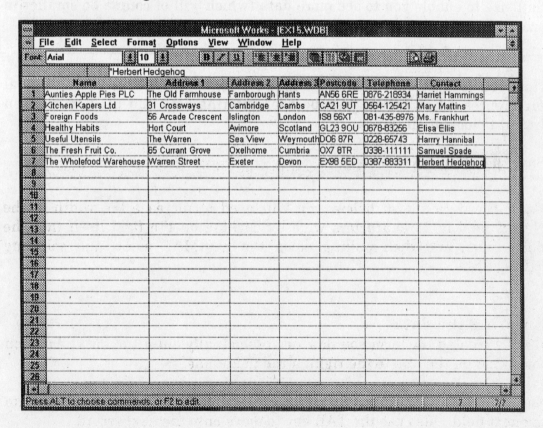

You may need to change the column widths as follows so that you can see all the data by clicking within each field and then using the FORMAT menu.

NAME	25
ADDRESS1	18
ADDRESS2	11
ADDRESS3	10
POSTCODE	10
TELEPHONE	12
CONTACT	16

Note :
If the data does not all fit onto the screen then you may need to alter the font size to enable you to see more data (which will of course be smaller in size).

How you look at the data will depend to some extent on your personal preferences; I find FORM view best for entering data and LIST view when I want to look at all the data.

Save the file as EX15.

Session 28: Adding data and sorting

Objectives

By the end of the session you will be able to :
Add data
Sort the data in various ways
Add headers and footers

Adding more data

Move back to FORM view by clicking on the FORM button in the toolbar and then CTRL END to move the cursor to the end of the file (a blank record should appear).

Make sure the cursor is at the beginning of the record (use the mouse or cursor keys to move it) and enter the following data.

Moorish Mouthfulls	Standway	The Saltings	Weymouth	DO7 65R	0228-43561	Merry Gerning
Live Yoghurt Co	33b Central Avenue	Barking	London	BA4 6T	071-345-6549	Judith Frames

Now switch back to LIST view and you should see the new record appear at the end of the list.

Now save the file as EX15.

Sorting the data into order

You will want to organise your data in various ways. You may want to sort it into some sort of order.

Using the file EX15, make sure you are in LIST view by clicking on the LIST button.

This time you are going to sort it into alphabetical order of name.

To do this pull down the SELECT menu followed by SORT RECORDS and you will see the following dialog box.

> Version 3, use the TOOLS menu rather than the SELECT menu.

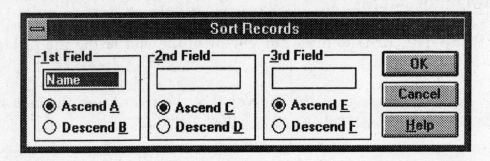

You can sort records by up to three fields. The first field is the primary field (the most important), the second field the secondary field and so on. Each field can be sorted in ascending or descending order.

This time make sure that the 1st Field says NAME (alter it if necessary) and click on OK. The datafile will be automatically reorganised into alphabetical order by the name of the supplier.

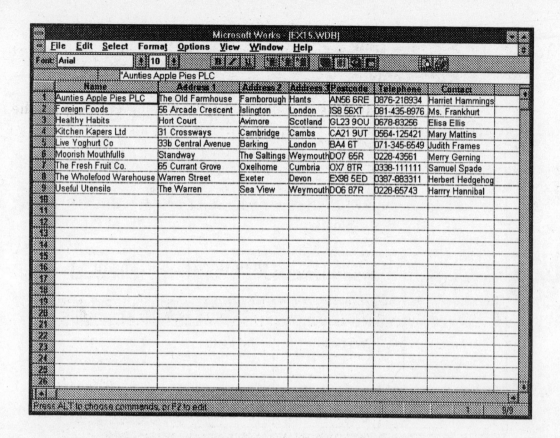

Sorting on multiple fields

The previous sort was using a single field, to sort on multiple fields is just as easy.

You are going to sort the data into ADDRESS 3 order and within that by ADDRESS 2.

Choose SELECT again and then SORT RECORDS and this time enter ADDRESS 3 in the 1st FIELD and ADDRESS 2 in the 2nd FIELD, then click on OK.

See how the data has been reorganised so that the data in ADDRESS 3 is in order and within that order the data is in order of ADDRESS 2.

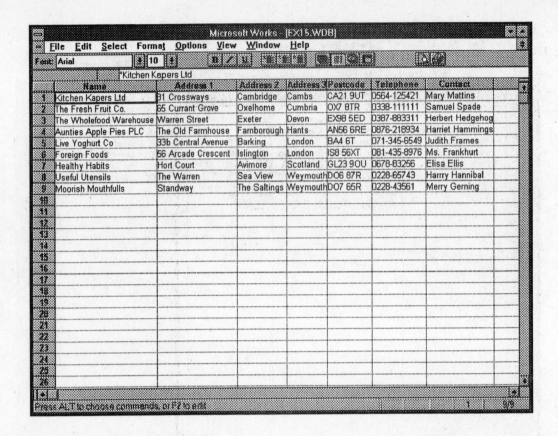

Adding headers and footers

Open the file EX15 and make sure you are in LIST view by clicking on the
LIST button.

Pull down the EDIT menu and select HEADERS & FOOTERS. This
operates in exactly the same way as within the spreadsheet module.

Version 3 choose the VIEW menu not the EDIT menu.

Enter your name as the header and the date as the footer.

Make sure that the PRINTER SETUP is set to PORTRAIT and that you
have chosen PORTRAIT in PAGE SETUP as well.

Click on the PREVIEW button on the toolbar and you will see it look like this.

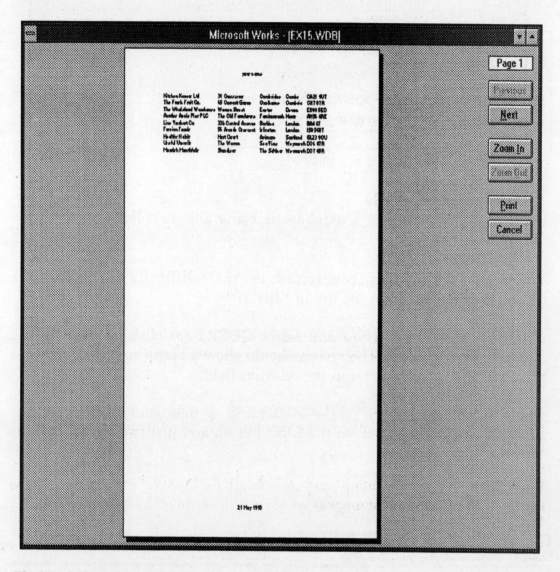

Click on the PRINTER button in the toolbar and print out your work.

Save it as EX15 and close it.

Session 29: Looking at the data

Objectives

By the end of the session you will be able to :
Interrogate the file in various ways

Interrogating the file

One of the attractions of a database is being able to select data from the entire file.

You want to display only those records in WEYMOUTH. To do this open the file EX15 and make sure you are in LIST view.

Pull down the VIEW menu and select QUERY (or click on the QUERY button in the toolbar). The screen should show a blank record. You enter the data you are looking for in the relevant field.

Enter the word (below) in the ADDRESS 3 field and then press the RETURN key. Then click on the LIST button and just two records will be shown.

Weymouth

In version 3 you will see a new dialog box appear when you click on the QUERY button in the toolbar. Alter the field name by clicking on the arrow to the right side of the field name box and select the field you want. Then enter the data you are looking for in the box to the right of the screen and click on APPLY NOW.

To get all the records shown again choose SELECT and SHOW ALL RECORDS.

Version 3 select the VIEW menu and then SHOW ALL RECORDS.

Note :
You may have to use the PAGE UP key or click on the scroll bar (on the right of the screen) to display all the records from the start of the file.

More sophisticated searching

You can search on more than one field simply by entering data into two or more fields within the QUERY screen. Click on the QUERY button in the toolbar. Remove the original data by highlighting and deleting it.

This time use the QUERY screen to display all the records in ISLINGTON (ADDRESS 2)and LONDON (ADDRESS 3) (you should end up with only one record displayed). When you have done this show all the records again.

There are various ways you can look at the data, some are described below.

>"G"   this will display all records with the first letter (or higher i.e. later in the alphabet) than G (in that field)

T*   displays all the records beginning with the letter T (the * symbol is called a wild card and means any additional characters)

<40   this will display all records lower than 40

>"S"&<"U"   all records between SA and TZ

Experiment to see how the Query works.

Be careful with search patterns as you can produce unexpected results if you are careless.

To practice this try to display the records where the ADDRESS 3 data begins with a letter greater than L.

See how in this example the firms in LONDON are shown as, in alphabetic terms, LO comes after L.

If that was successful display all the records where ADDRESS 3 data is between D and K.

Finally display all those records where the postcode is greater than C and the telephone number begins with a number greater than 03 (N.B. the query for the telephone number has to be included in speech marks - it is not considered a number as it contains a dash).

The result should look like this.

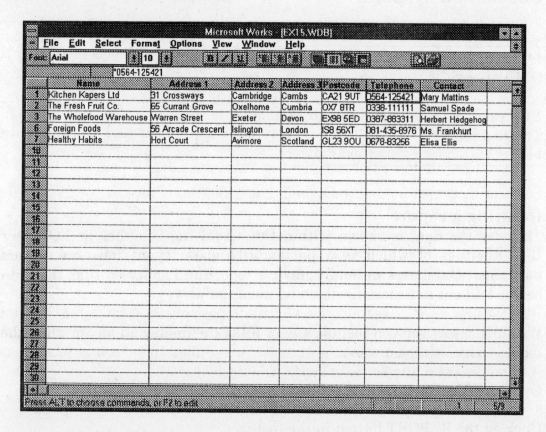

Finally close the file after saving the changes.

Session 30: Reports

Objectives

By the end of the session you will be able to :
Create a report

Creating a report

The way the data is shown within the actual file is either in FORM or LIST, neither of which is a particularly good layout for presentation purposes. Databases normally have a reporting facility so that the data can be laid out in a more flexible and meaningful way.

Within a report you can include any or all of the fields and any or all of the data, in any order you want.

Open the file EX15.

Click on the REPORT button in the toolbar.

This starts a series of questions which enable you to easily create your own individual report format.

The initial dialog box is shown below.

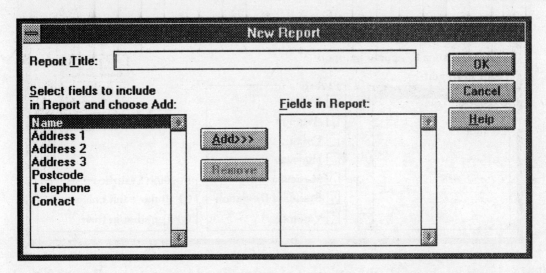

For this exercise the report title is (do not **Return** after entering it)

You enter a title for your report and then select the fields you want within the report by clicking on each field and then on the ADD button. When you have finished click on OK.

You are going to include the Name, Postcode, Telephone and Contact fields only.

This brings up another dialog box.

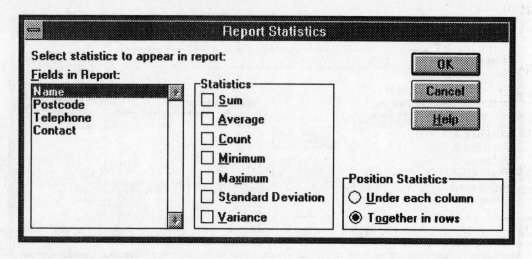

This is most useful when using numeric data as it allows you to automatically produce statistics from your data.

For this exercise simply click on OK without selecting any statistics.

Another dialog box appears telling you that the process is finished and you can see the result by clicking on the PREVIEW button in the toolbar. Click on OK.

At this point the actual format of the report is displayed and you can add to this or delete from it anything you want.

	A	B	C	D
Title			Customer List	
Title				
Headings	Name	Postcode	Telephone	Contact
Headings				
Record	='Name '	='Postcode	='Telephone '	='Contact '
Summary				

In this example highlight the headings and turn off the underlining by clicking on the underline button in the toolbar.

Now add another title in the second title row (underneath the original title),

Fiona's Food Ltd

and format it to bold.

Now position the cursor in row 3 and, using the EDIT menu, INSERT another title row (to create a space between the titles and headings).

Version 3 uses the INSERT menu not the EDIT menu.

Highlight the heading, (name, postcode, telephone and contact) and align them to the left (using the LEFT button in the toolbar).

Widen the columns (column A to 28 and the other columns to 15 each).

Highlight the two titles and EDIT and CUT, then position the cursor in the top left cell and EDIT and PASTE (this will move the titles to a new position).

Add your name as the header and the date as the footer (using the EDIT menu) and preview it.

The finished report should look like this.

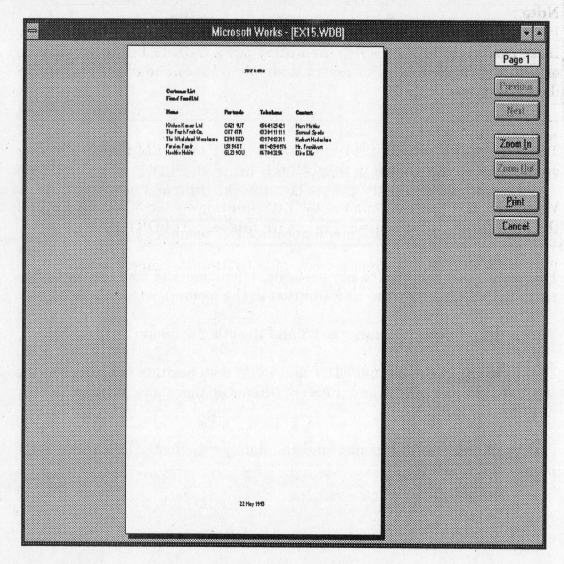

Now print your report and save the file as EX15.

Note :
If you want to include certain of the data in the report (for example, only those customers in LONDON), then carry out a QUERY before previewing or printing the report. The report is simply a **layout** to display whatever data you choose.

Try doing this (you will need to return to LIST or FORM first by clicking on the appropriate button in the toolbar).

When you have carried out the QUERY, pull down the VIEW menu and then select the report you want to use (in this case REPORT 1).

Preview it and if satisfactory close the file (**without** saving it again).

Grouping the data within a report
You may well want to group the data in some way within the report.

Open EX15 and then choose SELECT and SHOW ALL RECORDS.

VIEW your report.

Now choose SELECT and SORT RECORDS. The following dialog box will appear.

In version 3 use the TOOLS menu not the SELECT menu.

This time enter the fieldname ADDRESS 3 into the 1st FIELD box, then click on BREAK G (this groups the data according to the chosen field and puts a line break between each group).

When you have finished you will see that there are some entries in the SUM ADDRESS row. This adds the number of items in each group and can be deleted if you do not want this information. In this case it is unnecessary so highlight the data in that row and EDIT CLEAR.

Now PREVIEW the report and see how the data is sorted and grouped.

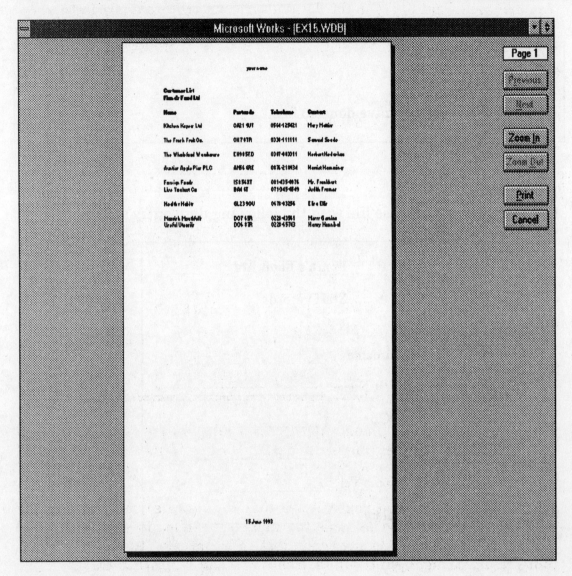

Save the file as EX15 and close it.

Session 31: Exercise

Objectives

To revise the work you have done so far.

Tasks

1. Create a new database file with the following data entry screen.

> **Fiona's Food Ltd**
>
> **Staff records**
>
> Surname   : ....
>
> First Name : ....
>
> DOB   : ....
>
> Sex   : ....
>
> Home Tel : ....
>
> Salary   : ....

2. Format the DOB field to TIME/DATE (FORMAT menu), choose MONTH, DAY, YEAR and select LONG, then format it to the left.

In version 3 choose FORMAT then NUMBER and choose the date format you want.

3. Align the SEX field to the left.

4.   Format the SALARY field to CURRENCY (2 decimal places).

5.   Now enter the following data into the file and then save it as EX16.

Jules	Julia	12 March 1949	F	0932-34591	£9,800.00
Melldraw	Melissa	04 December 1967	F	0870-23418	£12,500.00
Martins	Matthew	03 August 1956	M	0879-76581	£11,000.00
Hawkins	Harry	18 March 1934	M	0456-23871	£14,005.00
Suitings	Sally	10 April 1971	F	0934-21345	£5,602.00

6.   Click on the LIST VIEW button and alter the column widths so that they are of suitable widths and the data is displayed satisfactorily.

7.   Sort the data into order of SEX and within that into SURNAME order.

The result should look similar to this.

8. Add your name as the footer and the date as the header and preview the file.

9. If it is satisfactory then print it out.

10. Create a new report from the data (give the report the title WAGES REPORT) using the following fields in this order.

Surname
First Name
Sex
DOB
Salary

11. For the SALARY field include the following statistics in your report.

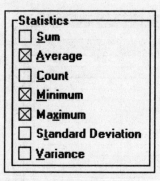

```
┌Statistics─────────────┐
│ ☐ Sum                 │
│ ☒ Average             │
│ ☐ Count               │
│ ☒ Minimum             │
│ ☒ Maximum             │
│ ☐ Standard Deviation  │
│ ☐ Variance            │
└───────────────────────┘
```

12. Alter the width of the columns in the report so that it looks well spaced.

13. Remove the underlining from the headings and align the headings to the left (except for the SALARY which should be right aligned).

14. Make sure that there is a blank line underneath the title and that the title is to the left of the report and that it is in bold.

15. Add your name and date as the footer (with space between them).

16. Sort the data into order of SEX and within that into order of SALARY.

The final report should look similar to this when previewed.

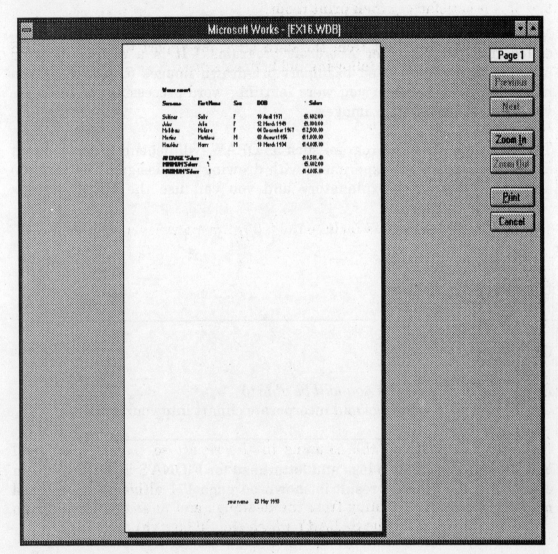

17. Save the file as EX16 and print it out.

18. Close the file.

Draw

MICROSOFT DRAW is a 'applet', a small application program that can be called from within other Microsoft programs. It is a simple drawing program that can be used to import pre-drawn images (clip art), as you have already done when you were learning word-processing, or to create your own logos and other images.

The use you make of a program such as DRAW will depend to some extent on your willingness to experiment with drawing and design. The menu(s) are more or less self-explanatory and you can use the HELP screens whenever necessary.

Session 32: Draw

Objectives

By the end of this session you will be able to :
Create your own drawings and incorporate clipart into your work

---

You are going to create a logo and letterhead for FIONA'S FOODS LTD (an example of the finished result is shown on page 171 although yours need not look identical).

Starting Off

Create a new word processing file and then choose INSERT and then DRAWING.

MICROSOFT DRAW will appear. Make this full screen so that you can see what you are doing more easily by clicking on the up arrow in the top right of the DRAW window.

The Tools

There are various tools available within DRAW and they are described below.

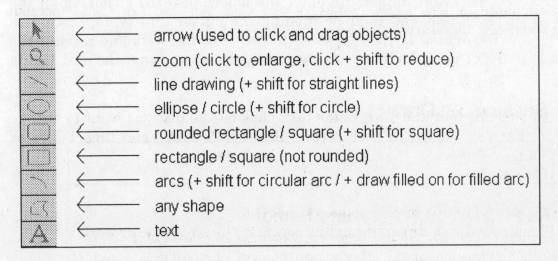

←	arrow (used to click and drag objects)
←	zoom (click to enlarge, click + shift to reduce)
←	line drawing (+ shift for straight lines)
←	ellipse / circle (+ shift for circle)
←	rounded rectangle / square (+ shift for square)
←	rectangle / square (not rounded)
←	arcs (+ shift for circular arc / + draw filled on for filled arc)
←	any shape
←	text

Using the tools

Select the tool you want by clicking on the tool.

Click the mouse wherever you want to begin to use any drawing tool and drag the mouse to draw the object. Then release the mouse when you have finished. This does not apply to the text tool where you simply click where you want to type and then type the text.

Creating a logo / letterhead
You are going to do this in stages.

1.	Import a picture from the clipart library (FILE then IMPORT PICTURE) as you did when word processing (remember to select the clipart directory so that the list of clipart files is shown). The file you want is VICHOUSE.WMF (although if using version 3 you will have to choose another).

	Move the picture up the screen by clicking on it and then dragging it.

2.	Underneath the picture enter the following text by clicking on the TEXT icon and then positioning the cursor and typing each line (**Return**ing at the end of each line). For the next line reselect the TEXT icon and then click the cursor where you want the next text to go.

To alter the font and sizes of the text, click on the text you want to change so that dots appear at each corner, then select TEXT and then FONT or SIZE.

Text	Font / format
Fiona's Food Ltd	times new roman 24 point bold
99 Vicarage Street	times new roman 14 point italic bold
Oldtown-by-the-Sea	times new roman 14 point italic bold
Somerset	times new roman 14 point italic bold
TA32 5AT	times new roman 14 point italic bold
0826-32983	times new roman 14 point italic bold

Move the text so that it is lined up vertically by clicking on the line and then dragging the line of text to a new position.

Note :
You can select more than one line of text or image by clicking and dragging the arrow tool over them all.

Now draw a rounded rectangle around the picture and the text by selecting the rounded rectangle tool, clicking the mouse in the start position, dragging it and letting go when finished.

Change the line style for the rectangle by clicking on the rectangle (so that the four corners are shown) and then on the DRAW command and then on LINE STYLE. From the choices select 2 point.

After you have drawn the rectangle the picture and text may have disappeared; this is because the rectangle is in front of them.

To bring back the picture and text click on EDIT and then select SEND TO BACK; this sends the rectangle back and brings the picture and text to the front.

Note :
If the rectangle (or any image) needs to be changed in size simply click within the image so that the four corners of the object appear. Then click on any of the corners and drag the corner to a new position.

The end result could look like this.

Now click on the FILE command and then EXIT and RETURN TO WORD1.

Answer YES to the question about updating the file and the logo will be entered into your word processing document.

Unfortunately at present it is in the wrong place and far too large.

Click on the image and align it to the right, position the cursor to the right of the image and then return twice and set the alignment to justification for the rest of the page.

Click on the image again (use PAGE UP to see it if necessary) and select FORMAT and then PICTURE. Alter the size to 60% (both measurements).

Alter the margins of the file to the following (inches) by selecting FILE and then PAGE SETUP & MARGINS.

top	0.8"
bottom	0.8"
left	1.0"
right	1.0"

If you preview your file you should see the logo as shown below.

If you want to alter the image at any time double click quickly on the image and DRAW will be loaded automatically.

Save your file as EX14 and close it.

Integration

You have used the word processing, spreadsheet, database and drawing tools. Now we will integrate the two.

This section includes the following sessions:

Session 33: Integrating the spreadsheet with the word processor
Session 34: Integrating the database and the word processor

Session 33: Integrating the spreadsheet with the word processor

---

Objectives

By the end of this session you will be able to :
Combine word processed documents with a spreadsheet.

You are going to create a short report which will include a chart and figures from the spreadsheet. Create a new word processing file and enter the following text.

Memo

From :Harry
To   :Fiona

Here are the staff salary figures for the last six months. I have included both the figures and a bar chart showing the figures graphically.

The actual figures are:

Centre the title and format it to bold and two points larger than the rest of the text.

Format the words From and To in bold.

Return twice after the end of the text to create space.

Pasting the figures

Open the file EX10 and highlight all the figures and the text.

Pull down the EDIT menu and select COPY.

Pull down the WINDOW menu and select your new word processing file from the list.

Position the cursor where you want the figures to be displayed (after the text).

Pull down the EDIT menu again and select PASTE.

Highlight the figures and alter the font to COURIER NEW (Courier is a font which displays tables of numbers better than a font such as Times Roman).

Notes :

If the figures wrap around the screen then you have three options.

Alter the page margins (FILE and PAGE SETUP & MARGINS) to, say, 0.3" left and right.

Alter the font for the pasted data to a smaller size.

Go back to the spreadsheet and reduce the column widths then copy the data to the word processing file again.

Place a border around the figures.

Pasting the chart

Position the cursor below the figures and pull down the INSERT menu and select CHART.

Highlight the spreadsheet you want to use (in this case EX10) and a list of the available charts will appear. Click on the one you want to copy (CHART 2) and then click on OK. The chart should automatically appear.

Centre the chart on the page.

Add your name and the date as the footer and preview your work.

Note :
If you want to alter the size of the chart simply click on it and select FORMAT PICTURE and change the figures.

It should look similar to this.

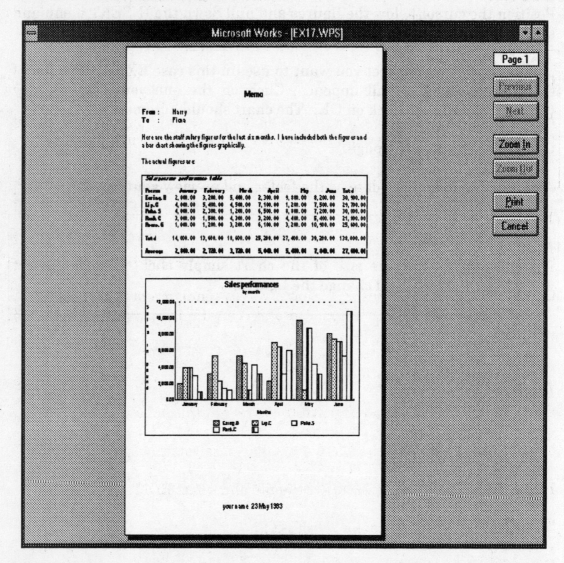

If you are happy with your work save it as EX17 and print it out and then close the files.

Session 34: Integrating the database and the word processor

Objectives

By the end of this session you will be able to :
Combine a word processed document with information from a database
Carry out a mail merge

There are two possibilities here.

☐ Pasting data from the database into a word processed document.

☐ Carrying out a mail-merge. This involves sending a standard letter to, say, your customers, which contains certain information specific to each.

Pasting data

Open up the file EX17 and position the cursor at the end of the file.

Open up your database file EX16 and make sure you are using LIST view.

Highlight the first four columns of the file and select EDIT and COPY.

Through the WINDOW menu select EX17.

Select EDIT and PASTE and the data should appear within your memo.

Draw a box around the data and indent the box by a 3" right indent.

Add a heading above the database material.

```
┌─────────────────────────────┐
│                             │
│ Employee records            │
│                             │
└─────────────────────────────┘
```

Format the heading to bold and make it two points larger than the rest of the text (align to the left).

You will probably find that your work now extends over two pages. Put a page break before the database material.

After the database names add the following text

```
┌─────────────────────────────┐
│                             │
│ I hope this is of use to you.│
│                             │
└─────────────────────────────┘
```

You may need to align this to the left and alter the fonts.

Add a page number as the header and preview your file.

If it is satisfactory then print it out.

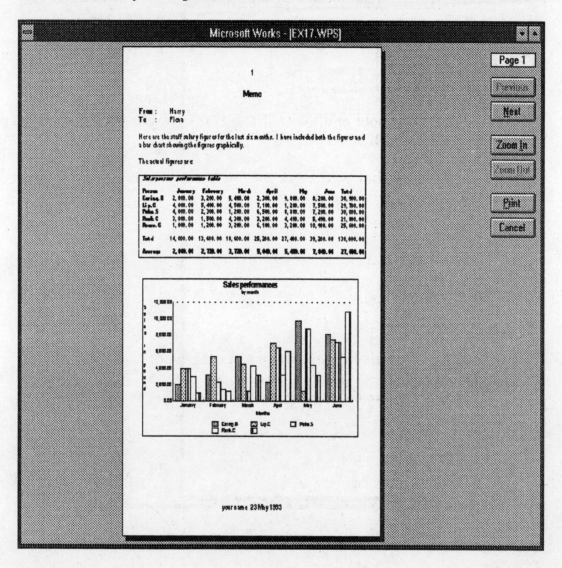

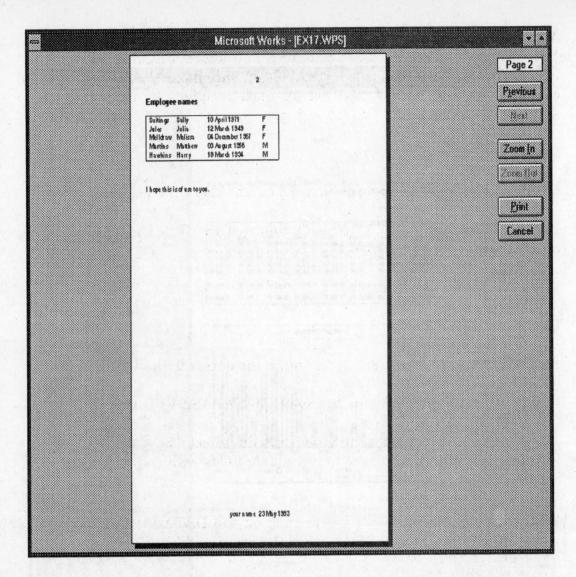

Save and close all the files.

Mail-merging

You are going to merge a list of names and address from a database file into a word processing file. Each letter will have the same standard contents but will be personalised for each recipient by being addressed specifically to them.

Open the database file EX15.

Open up the file EX14 and position the cursor below the logo.

Enter the current date by INSERT followed by SPECIAL CHARACTER and then click on PRINT DATE.

Align the date to the right.

Enter your name as a footer.

RETURN twice to create space and align the cursor to the left.

Pull down the INSERT menu and select DATABASE FIELD.

A dialog box will appear and you should select the database you are interested in (EX15). A list of the available fields within that database will be shown (see below).

Within version 3 you may have to click on the DATABASE button to the right of the dialog box and then select the required file.

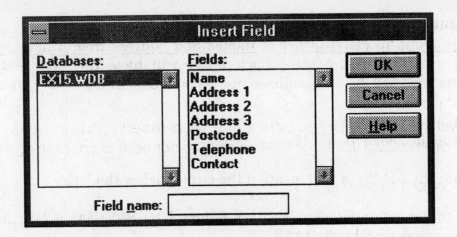

In this case select the following fields to insert.

Address 1
Address 2
Address 3
Postcode
Name

Please enter them as shown on the page 184 (remembering to RETURN onto a new line where necessary). You will need to repeat this process for each field.

Space out your letter and enter the following text.

Dear

I am writing to request your presence at a meeting to be held at our offices on the 23rd January 1994 to discuss our new product range.

I look forward to seeing you.

Yours Sincerely,

Fiona Fortescue

The final result should look like this.

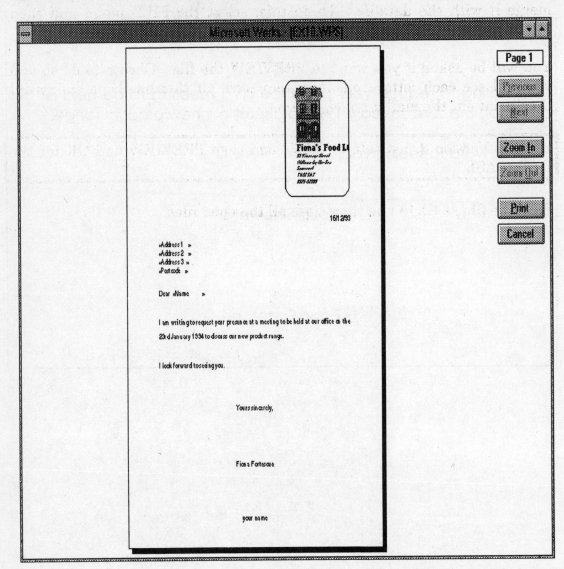

Now that you have created a standard letter all you now have to do is to merge it with the datafile. To do this, select the FILE menu and then PRINT FORM LETTERS.

You will be asked if you want to PREVIEW the file. Choose to do so and you will see each letter appear in sequence. If this has been successful then print out the mail merged letters.

> If using Version 3 just select PRINT and then PREVIEW and OK for the DATABASE.

Save the file as EX18 and then close all the open files.

Final exercises

These exercises are intended to bring together the various skills and commands you have learnt throughout the book.

If you need any assistance you have two sensible options:

Look back through the book for the section dealing with the task

or

Ask someone.

Objectives

To thoroughly revise the material you have covered in the book

---

Task one

You are going to create an advertisement for a running shop which has opened in your area.

The text that is needed is shown below.

The Runners Room
Old Street Arcade
Bobington
Berkshire
tel: 0345-14237
fax: 0345-18883

Open 9.30 - 5.00 Monday to Saturday

Special Opening Day 21/4/94

Karon Jones will be here to sign autographs of her book

Many offers on the day

The first 20 customers get a free pair of Nike socks

Add your name and the date as a footer.

There are two pictures that I have used called RUNNING.WMF and CROWD.WMF, however, there are many other pictures in the clipart library and you may decide to include others.

An example of how the finished advertisement could look is shown, but it is up to you to either copy the example or to design your own.

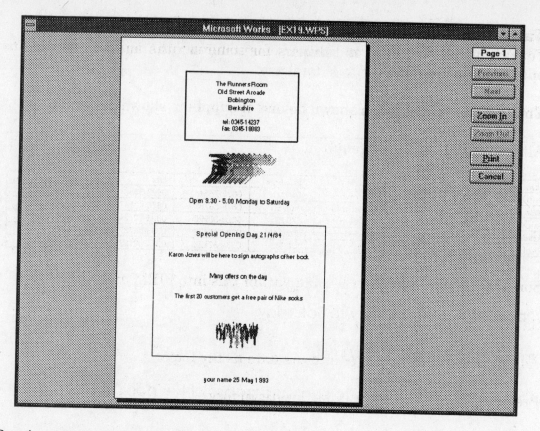

Preview your work and when you are satisfied, save it as EX19 and print it.

Task two

Your firm has now been in business for some months and has decided to put the list of suppliers onto a database.

Create a database file and enter the list of suppliers shown below.

Alter the field widths as required.

Firm	Address	Town	Postcode	Phone	Fax	Contact
Imp Sport	78 Higher Kyde	Oldtown	NT4 9MN	0823-76546	0823-54321	Gareth Gardens
Nike Ltd.	The Old Mills	Newcastle	DH65 8UY	0878-56789	0878-43567	Sally Dunkins
Asics	43 The Heights	Oldtown	NT78 TR4	0823-00998	0823-32121	Manuel Polits
Adidas PLC	99 Strengthways	Stratford	WO98 67T	0333-45678	0333-56789	Merry Martins
Reebok Ltd	President Park	Newtown	NT78 9IU	0234-32123	0234-32123	Peter Parkins

Sort the file into TOWN order and within this into FIRM order.

Save the file as EX20A.

Add your name as a header and the date as the footer.

Preview the file and print it out if satisfactory.

Task three

Using the file EX20A, create a report with the following heading

```
Suppliers List
```

and include only these fields,

```
Firm
Postcode
Telephone
Contact
```

do not include any statistics.

Cut and paste the title to the top left of the report and left align and remove the underlining of the headings.

Enter your name and the date as the footer.

Preview this and print out if satisfactory.

Save it as EX20A.

The result should look like this.

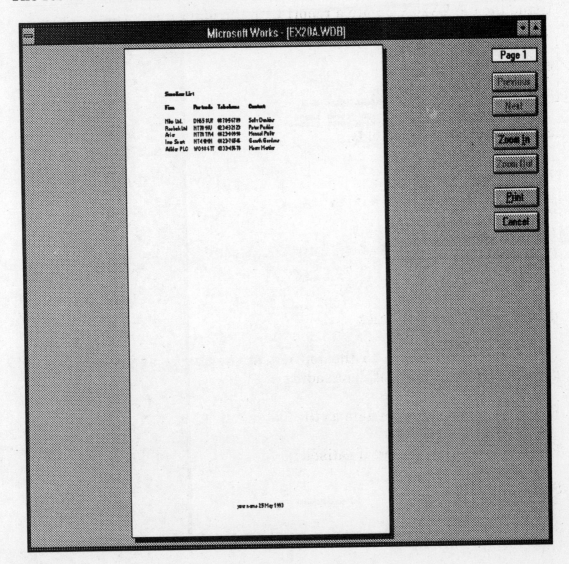

Now return to the database and set up a query so that only the firms in OLDTOWN are shown.

Print out the report again using the queried database file.

The new report should look like this.

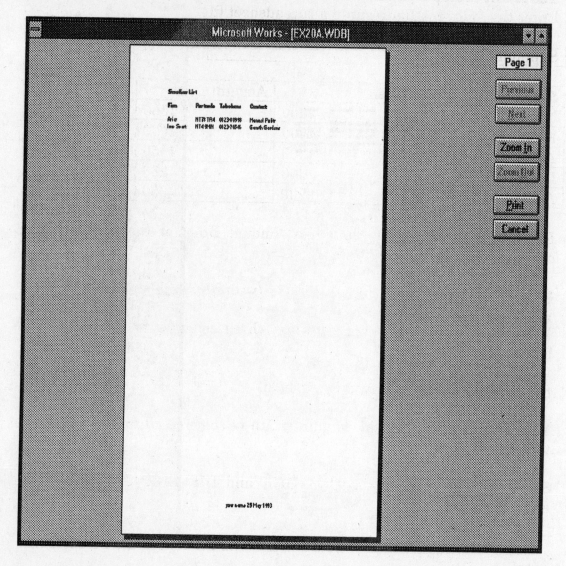

Show all the records again and close the file after saving it as EX20A.

Task four

Enter the following figures into a spreadsheet file.

Suppliers Credit Listing

Supplier	Credit Limit	Amount Due	Difference
Nike	2000	1500	
Reebock	1500	1600	
Asics	1200	1350	
Imp Sport	350	200	
Adidas	900	350	

Enter a formula (Credit Limit less Amount Due) for the DIFFERENCE column and fill it down.

Format all the numbers to CURRENCY (with **no** decimal places).

Make sure that you format the last three columns to the right (both headings and figures).

Format the two rows of headings to bold.

You may need to alter the column width of some or all of the columns so that all the data is displayed.

SUM the total of the AMOUNT DUE and DIFFERENCE columns and enter the word

Total

in the first column. Format the figures to currency (no decimal places).

Insert a blank line between the last supplier and the total row.

Sort the supplier names into alphabetical order.

Put a border around all the data and enter your name as the header and the date as the footer.

Preview your work and if it is satisfactory print it out.

The end result should look similar to this.

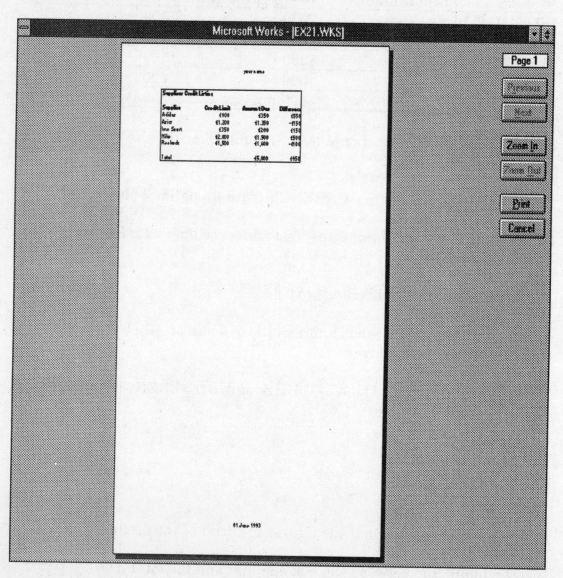

Save the file as EX21 and close it.

Task five
Open the file EX21.

Create a bar chart of the data (do not include the TOTAL row).

Add titles (including your name) to your chart and alter the fonts to give the most professional layout.

Add horizontal gridlines to your chart.

Display the chart as printed and alter the patterns and colours to give the best result.

Add a border to your chart and then add the date as a header.

Change the orientation to landscape.

Preview the file and, if it is satisfactory, print it out.

It may look similar to this.

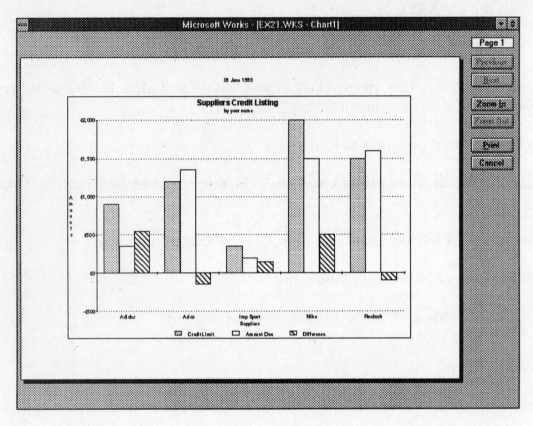

Save it as EX21.

Duplicate the chart so that you have two identical charts.

Now view the second chart and alter it to a line graph with both vertical and horizontal grid lines.

Alter the patterns and colours so that each line on the graph is different to look at and the markers are also distinct from each other.

Again preview this and print it out. The result may look like this.

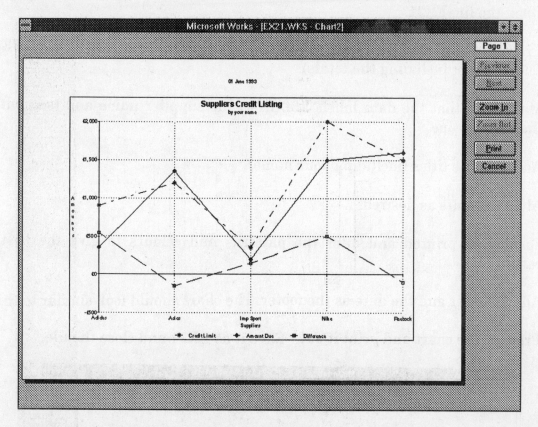

Save your work as EX21 and close the file.

final exercises

Task six
Open the file EX21.

Create an exploded pie chart of just the SUPPLIER and AMOUNT DUE columns (not including the totals).

Make sure that the data labels are (first) the supplier name and (second) the amount due.

Add suitable titles (including your name).

Alter the fonts as desired.

Display as printed and alter the patterns and colours to give the best result.

Add a border and the date as the footer. The chart should look similar to this.

Preview the chart and print it out. Save it as EX21 and close the file.

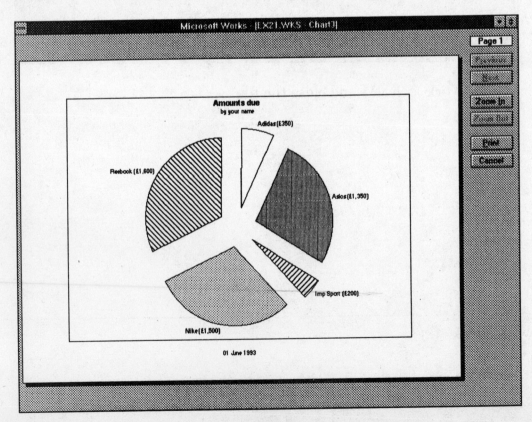

Task seven

You are going to mail-merge certain of your suppliers.

Open the database file EX20A.

Create a logo/letterhead for the RUNNERS ROOM. The logo/letterhead should incorporate the address and name of the firm as well as any graphics you may wish to create (using DRAW) or any piece of clipart.

Add to the letterhead the fields for the suppliers names and addresses from EX20A; look at the example on the next page for the suggested layout.

Add the following text to your letter, ensuring that it is justified and spell checked.

As you can see from the chart and figures (shown below) the credit limit you have given us is different to other firms with which we deal.

We would like you to reconsider the credit limit which we have with you so that we are able to trade with you effectively.

Yours sincerely,

your name

Insert the first bar chart you produced (EX21) and size it to 70% (height and width) and centre it.

Copy the spreadsheet data itself into your letter and put a double line border around it.

Put a page break between the chart and the figures.

The letter will begin to look something like this.

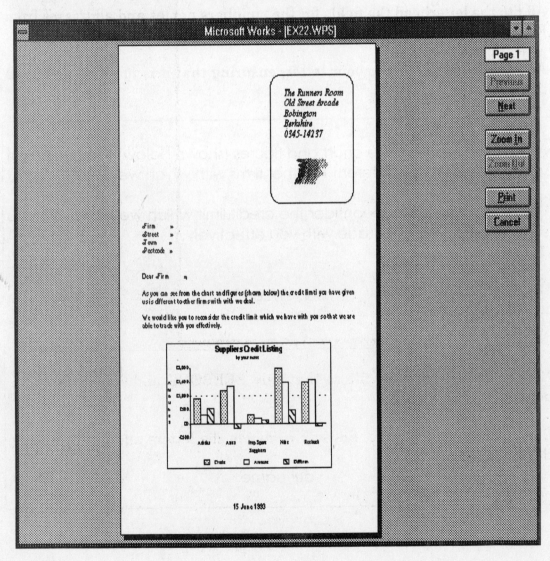

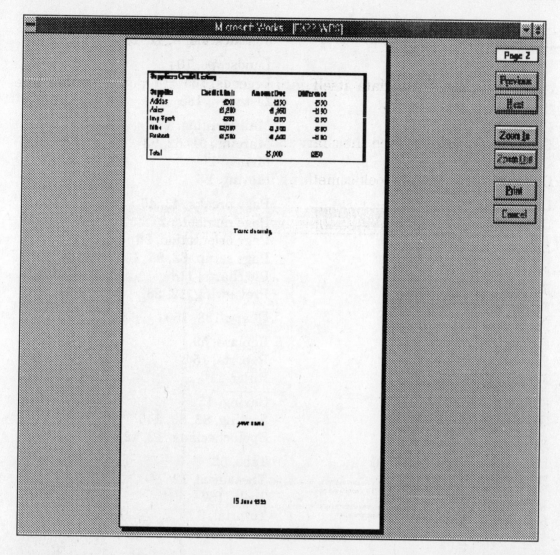

Now query the database file so that only REEBOCK and ASICS are mail merged.

Carry out the mail merge, firstly previewing the letters and then printing them out.

Save the file as EX22 and close it.

Index